A Journey
with Matthew

The 50 Day Bible Challenge

Cover design: Albonetti Design

This collection © 2014 Marek P. Zabriskie

Individual essays are the property of the authors.

All rights reserved.

ISBN: 978-0-88028-383-0

Printed in USA

Forward Movement
412 Sycamore Street
Cincinnati, OH 45202-4195
www.forwardmovement.org

A Journey
with Matthew

The 50 Day Bible Challenge

Edited by Marek P. Zabriskie

FORWARD MOVEMENT
Cincinnati, Ohio

Introduction

The Bible Challenge began as a simple idea: to encourage daily reading of scripture. Simple ideas, however, are often the ones that bring forth great change. Today, more than 100,000 people in 2,500 churches in over forty countries participate in The Bible Challenge. The initiative encourages individuals, churches, and dioceses to read the entire Bible in a year. We also offer opportunities to read the New Testament, Psalms, and Proverbs.

We continue our partnership with Forward Movement with a new series—a focus on reading one book of the Bible over a fifty-day period. This Bible Challenge series offers an ideal resource for individuals, churches, and dioceses for use during Eastertide or other times of the year.

The Bible remains the world's best-selling book year after year. While most Episcopalians, Roman Catholics, and mainline Christians have a Bible in their home, many of the books are gathering dust. Church historian and author Diana Butler Bass notes that of almost 22,000 Christian groups and denominations in the United States, Episcopalians are the best-educated Christian group in the country. But when it comes to biblical literacy, we drop almost to dead last.

The goal of The Bible Challenge is to help individuals develop a lifelong, daily spiritual discipline of reading the Bible so that their lives may be constantly transformed and renewed. Saint Augustine and many other great Christians have written about the power of reading the Bible quietly on our own. There is no other book in the world that can so transform the human heart, motivate the human spirit, and give us the mind that was in Christ Jesus himself.

Studies reveal that regular engagement with the Bible is the single best way to develop a strong Christian faith. It enhances our experience of worship and helps to create a more committed, articulate, and contagious Christian. This is exactly what the world needs today.

With prayers and blessings for your faithful Bible reading,

The Rev. Marek P. Zabriskie
Rector of St. Thomas Episcopal Church
Fort Washington, Pennsylvania
Founder and director of the
Center for Biblical Studies
www.thecenterforbiblicalstudies.org

How to Read the Bible Prayerfully

Welcome to The 50 Day Bible Challenge. We are delighted that you are interested in reading God's life-transforming Word from the Gospel of Matthew. It will change and enrich your life. Here are some suggestions to consider as you get started:

- You can begin The 50 Day Bible Challenge at any time of the year that you desire. It works especially well for the fifty days of Eastertide, beginning on Easter Day. It also could be read during Lent, beginning on the Sunday before Ash Wednesday.

- Each day has a manageable amount of reading, a meditation, a question or two, and a prayer, written by a host of wonderful authors.

- We suggest that you try to read the Bible each day. It is a great spiritual discipline to establish.

- If, however, you need more than fifty days to read through the Gospel of Matthew, we support you in moving at the pace that works best for you.

- Many Bible Challenge participants read the Bible using their iPad, iPhone, Kindle, or Nook, or listen to the Bible on CDs or on a mobile device using Audio.com, faithcomesthroughhearing.org, or Pandora radio. Find what works for you.

- Our website at www.thecenterforbiblicalresources.org offers a list of resources, if you desire to learn more about the Bible. We also offer a Read the Bible in a Year program and a Read the New Testament, Psalms, and Proverbs in a Year reading plans as well.

- Because the Bible is not a newspaper, it is best to read it with a reverent spirit. We advocate a devotional approach to reading the Bible, rather than reading it as a purely intellectual or academic exercise.

- Before reading the Bible, take a moment of silence to put yourself in the presence of God. We then invite you to read this prayer written by Archbishop Thomas Cranmer.

   Blessed Lord, who has caused all holy scriptures to be written for our learning: Grant us to hear them, read, mark, learn, and inwardly digest them, that we may embrace and ever hold fast the blessed hope of everlasting life, which you have given us in our Savior Jesus Christ; who lives and reigns with you and the Holy Spirit, one God, for ever and ever. Amen.

- Consider using the ancient monastic practice of *lectio divina*. In this form of Bible reading, you read the text and then meditate on a portion of it—be it a verse or two or even a single word. Mull over the words and their meaning. Then offer a prayer to God based on what you have read and how it has made you feel or what it has caused you to ponder. Listen in silence for God to respond to your prayer.

- We encourage you to read in the morning, if possible, so that your prayerful reading may spiritually enliven the rest of your day. If you cannot read in the morning, read when you can later in the day. Try to carve out a regular time for your daily reading.

- One way to hold yourself accountable to reading God's Word is to form a group within your church or community. By participating in The 50 Day Bible Challenge together, you can support one another in your reading, discuss the Bible passages, ask questions, and share how God's Word is transforming your life.

- If you do not want to join a group, you may wish to invite a friend or family member or two to share The 50 Day Bible Challenge with you.

- Put a notice in your church newsletter that you are starting a group to participate in The 50 Day Bible Challenge. Invite others to join you and to gather regularly to discuss the readings, ask questions, and share how it is transforming your life. Visit our website to see more resources for how churches can participate in The Bible Challenge.

- If you form a Bible Challenge group, consider holding a gathering or meal to celebrate your spiritual accomplishment.

- Have fun and find spiritual peace and the joy that God desires for you in your daily reading. The goal of the Center for Biblical Studies is to help you discover God's wisdom and to create a lifelong spiritual practice of daily Bible reading so that God may guide you through each day of your life.

- If you find reading the entire Bible and being part of The Bible Challenge to be a blessing in your life, then we strongly encourage you to share the blessing. Invite several friends or family members to participate in The Bible Challenge.

- Once you've finished one complete reading of the Bible, start over and do it again. God may speak differently to you in each reading. Follow the example of U.S. President John Adams, who read through the Bible each year during his adult life. We highly advocate this practice.

- After participating in The 50 Day Bible Challenge, you will be more able to support and mentor others in reading the Bible.

We are thrilled that you are participating in The Bible Challenge. May God richly bless you as you prayerfully engage the scriptures each day.

A Journey
with Matthew

The 50 Day Bible Challenge

Matthew 1:1-25

1 An account of the genealogy of Jesus the Messiah, the son of David, the son of Abraham. ²Abraham was the father of Isaac, and Isaac the father of Jacob, and Jacob the father of Judah and his brothers, ³and Judah the father of Perez and Zerah by Tamar, and Perez the father of Hezron, and Hezron the father of Aram, ⁴and Aram the father of Aminadab, and Aminadab the father of Nahshon, and Nahshon the father of Salmon, ⁵and Salmon the father of Boaz by Rahab, and Boaz the father of Obed by Ruth, and Obed the father of Jesse, ⁶and Jesse the father of King David. And David was the father of Solomon by the wife of Uriah, ⁷and Solomon the father of Rehoboam, and Rehoboam the father of Abijah, and Abijah the father of Asaph, ⁸and Asaph the father of Jehoshaphat, and Jehoshaphat the father of Joram, and Joram the father of Uzziah, ⁹and Uzziah the father of Jotham, and Jotham the father of Ahaz, and Ahaz the father of Hezekiah, ¹⁰and Hezekiah the father of Manasseh, and Manasseh the father of Amos, and Amos the father of Josiah, ¹¹and Josiah the father of Jechoniah and his brothers, at the time of the deportation to Babylon. ¹²And after the deportation to Babylon: Jechoniah was the father of Salathiel, and Salathiel the father of Zerubbabel, ¹³and Zerubbabel the father of Abiud, and Abiud the father of Eliakim, and Eliakim the father of Azor, ¹⁴and Azor the father of Zadok, and Zadok the father of Achim, and Achim the father of Eliud, ¹⁵and Eliud the father of Eleazar, and Eleazar the father of Matthan, and Matthan the

father of Jacob, [16]and Jacob the father of Joseph the husband of Mary, of whom Jesus was born, who is called the Messiah. [17]So all the generations from Abraham to David are fourteen generations; and from David to the deportation to Babylon, fourteen generations; and from the deportation to Babylon to the Messiah, fourteen generations.

[18]Now the birth of Jesus the Messiah took place in this way. When his mother Mary had been engaged to Joseph, but before they lived together, she was found to be with child from the Holy Spirit. [19]Her husband Joseph, being a righteous man and unwilling to expose her to public disgrace, planned to dismiss her quietly. [20]But just when he had resolved to do this, an angel of the Lord appeared to him in a dream and said, "Joseph, son of David, do not be afraid to take Mary as your wife, for the child conceived in her is from the Holy Spirit. [21]She will bear a son, and you are to name him Jesus, for he will save his people from their sins." [22]All this took place to fulfill what had been spoken by the Lord through the prophet: [23]"Look, the virgin shall conceive and bear a son, and they shall name him Emmanuel," which means, "God is with us." [24]When Joseph awoke from sleep, he did as the angel of the Lord commanded him; he took her as his wife, [25]but had no marital relations with her until she had borne a son; and he named him Jesus.

Reflection

Most people want to skip the genealogy. A long list of names does not make for riveting reading. However, we are all interested in our past. One of the most searched-for items on the Internet is around our personal ancestry. We are curious to know where we come from, who preceded us, and who shaped us into the people we are today.

And so the Gospel of Matthew starts with a genealogy. This is the genealogy of Jesus the Messiah (the anointed one; in Greek, the Christ). It is an extraordinary group. Most of those listed are men, with their fair share of complexities. Interestingly, only five women are listed: Tamar, Rahab, Ruth, Bathsheba, and Mary (the mother of Jesus). These are remarkable women. Tamar dresses as a prostitute to seduce Judah and maintain the familial line (Genesis 38); Rahab is the "harlot" who hid the Jewish spies (Joshua 2). Ruth is the Moabitess who married into the Jewish line; and Bathsheba is the famous wife of Uriah—the object of King David's lust and ultimately the person he makes pregnant (2 Samuel 11-12).

So how does God work in the world? We learn from this genealogy that God takes our complex lives and allows grace to emerge. It is not that God approves of King David's seduction of Bathsheba (and ultimate murder of Uriah), but even our depravity cannot stop the purposes of God. Often God's providence can only be seen in retrospect. As we look back, we can see God's grace—and discover hope.

The Very Rev. Ian S. Markham, PhD
Dean and President of Virginia Theological Seminary
Alexandria, Virginia

Question _____

Reflect on your life. Look back at the hard and difficult times. How did God's grace create a pattern for hope?

Prayer _____

Loving God, take our broken lives and use them for your grace. Help us in the difficult times to trust that a pattern of hope will emerge; and help us to look back with gratitude on the way your loving embrace held us and created a presence of hope. In Jesus' name. Amen.

Matthew 2:1-23

2 In the time of King Herod, after Jesus was born in Bethlehem of Judea, wise men from the East came to Jerusalem, ²asking, "Where is the child who has been born king of the Jews? For we observed his star at its rising, and have come to pay him homage." ³When King Herod heard this, he was frightened, and all Jerusalem with him; ⁴and calling together all the chief priests and scribes of the people, he inquired of them where the Messiah was to be born. ⁵They told him, "In Bethlehem of Judea; for so it has been written by the prophet: ⁶'And you, Bethlehem, in the land of Judah, are by no means least among the rulers of Judah; for from you shall come a ruler who is to shepherd my people Israel.'" ⁷Then Herod secretly called for the wise men and learned from them the exact time when the star had appeared. ⁸Then he sent them to Bethlehem, saying, "Go and search diligently for the child; and when you have found him, bring me word so that I may also go and pay him homage."

⁹When they had heard the king, they set out; and there, ahead of them, went the star that they had seen at its rising, until it stopped over the place where the child was. ¹⁰When they saw that the star had stopped, they were overwhelmed with joy. ¹¹On entering the house, they saw the child with Mary his mother; and they knelt down and paid him homage. Then, opening their treasure chests, they offered him gifts of gold, frankincense, and myrrh. ¹²And having been warned in a dream not to return to Herod, they left for their own country by another road.

¹³Now after they had left, an angel of the Lord appeared to Joseph in a dream and said, "Get up, take the child and his mother, and flee to Egypt, and remain there until I tell you; for Herod is about to search for the child, to destroy him." ¹⁴Then Joseph got up, took the child and his mother by night, and went to Egypt, ¹⁵and remained there until the death of Herod. This was to fulfill what had been spoken by the Lord through the prophet, "Out of Egypt I have called my son."

¹⁶When Herod saw that he had been tricked by the wise men, he was infuriated, and he sent and killed all the children in and around Bethlehem who were two years old or under, according to the time that he had learned from the wise men. ¹⁷Then was fulfilled what had been spoken through the prophet Jeremiah: ¹⁸"A voice was heard in Ramah, wailing and loud lamentation, Rachel weeping for her children; she refused to be consoled, because they are no more."

¹⁹When Herod died, an angel of the Lord suddenly appeared in a dream to Joseph in Egypt and said, ²⁰"Get up, take the child and his mother, and go to the land of Israel, for those who were seeking the child's life are dead." ²¹Then Joseph got up, took the child and his mother, and went to the land of Israel. ²²But when he heard that Archelaus was ruling over Judea in place of his father Herod, he was afraid to go there. And after being warned in a dream, he went away to the district of Galilee. ²³There he made his home in a town called Nazareth, so that what had been spoken through the prophets might be fulfilled, "He will be called a Nazorean."

Reflection

It is amazing. The incarnation of God is a young child. And this young child is dependent on young parents to keep him safe (Jewish women at this time would have been married as they reached puberty, so Mary is probably no more than fourteen). The power and political structures of the day are challenged by the disclosure of God in their midst. The wise men represent power that recognizes this disclosure in a positive way; King Herod represents power that is fearful and resorts to brutal violence to crush this moment. This little child is caught in the vortex; this little child that Christians believe is God Incarnate has to navigate the challenge of human political structures.

The God we worship understands the complexity of human life and our relations with each other. The story of the Incarnation is a constant engagement with these powerful forces. But God is in control; the spiritual realm—through dreams and angels—connects with the physical realm to safeguard the promise embodied in this child. So a dream instructs the wise men to return to their own country on a route that bypasses Herod, and an angel of the Lord ensures that Joseph takes the child to safety in Egypt.

There is much in this narrative: two contrasting political responses, the miracle of the Incarnation dependent on young people, and the way in which the spiritual realm interconnects with the physical.

The Very Rev. Ian S. Markham, PhD
Dean and President of Virginia Theological Seminary
Alexandria, Virginia

Questions

Do you respond positively to the demands of love (like the wise men) or with fear (like Herod)?

What do you think about the miracle of a God that becomes a vulnerable child dependent on young parents?

Prayer

Holy One of light and love, we marvel and thank you for the miracle of the Incarnation. We thank you that you took human form and made yourself dependent on the judgment of young parents. We bow the knee and recognize that this is true love. Please help us to be agents of love, equally willing to be vulnerable and dependent on others. In Jesus' name. Amen.

Matthew 3:1-17

3 In those days John the Baptist appeared in the wilderness of Judea, proclaiming, ²"Repent, for the kingdom of heaven has come near." ³This is the one of whom the prophet Isaiah spoke when he said, "The voice of one crying out in the wilderness: 'Prepare the way of the Lord, make his paths straight.'" ⁴Now John wore clothing of camel's hair with a leather belt around his waist, and his food was locusts and wild honey. ⁵Then the people of Jerusalem and all Judea were going out to him, and all the region along the Jordan, ⁶and they were baptized by him in the river Jordan, confessing their sins.

⁷But when he saw many Pharisees and Sadducees coming for baptism, he said to them, "You brood of vipers! Who warned you to flee from the wrath to come? ⁸Bear fruit worthy of repentance. ⁹Do not presume to say to yourselves, 'We have Abraham as our ancestor'; for I tell you, God is able from these stones to raise up children to Abraham. ¹⁰Even now the ax is lying at the root of the trees; every tree therefore that does not bear good fruit is cut down and thrown into the fire. ¹¹"I baptize you with water for repentance, but one who is more powerful than I is coming after me; I am not worthy to carry his sandals. He will baptize you with the Holy Spirit and fire. ¹²His winnowing fork is in his hand, and he will clear his threshing floor and will gather his wheat into the granary; but the chaff he will burn with unquenchable fire."

¹³Then Jesus came from Galilee to John at the Jordan, to be

baptized by him. [14]John would have prevented him, saying, "I need to be baptized by you, and do you come to me?" [15]But Jesus answered him, "Let it be so now; for it is proper for us in this way to fulfill all righteousness." Then he consented. [16]And when Jesus had been baptized, just as he came up from the water, suddenly the heavens were opened to him and he saw the Spirit of God descending like a dove and alighting on him. [17]And a voice from heaven said, "This is my Son, the Beloved, with whom I am well pleased."

Reflection

John the Baptist appears on the stage of Matthew's Gospel dressed in the classic garb of a Hebrew prophet and eating locusts and wild honey (traditional prophet food). John is the culmination of the long line of prophets who have come before and whose words and witness have pointed to the coming of the Messiah.

However, if John appeared on our streets today dressed in this way, we might perceive him as a fringe person and a beggar rather than the final flower of the Hebrew prophetic tradition. Even in his own day, John was out on the fringe.

God appears to have a preference for appearing on the fringes of human life and history. No historical mention of the Israelite's exodus from slavery in Egypt has been found other than in scripture. As important as the prophets are to our tradition, they were not particularly newsworthy in their own day. Israel was a faraway and troublesome province of the Roman Empire. Jesus was born in an out-of-the-way town, and so on.

There is a distinct connection between God's appearing and beggars. Later in Matthew, Jesus says that giving a cup of water or a coat to a beggar or visiting a prisoner is in fact serving Jesus. That is, Jesus is making his appearance as the thirsty or naked or imprisoned. There is indeed a connection between seeing a beggar and encountering God. Seeing God in the beggar and the needy is a work of the heart. It takes practice to begin seeing the beggar. Indeed, a church without beggars is a museum.

The Rt. Rev. Clifton Daniel
Bishop of the Diocese of Pennsylvania
Philadelphia, Pennsylvania

Questions

Why is a church without beggars a museum?

Where are the beggars in your church?

Prayer

God, give us the grace and sight to see you in unexpected places. And give us the strength and courage to serve you when we see you in our neighbors. Amen.

Matthew 4:1-22

4 Then Jesus was led up by the Spirit into the wilderness to be tempted by the devil. ²He fasted forty days and forty nights, and afterwards he was famished. ³The tempter came and said to him, "If you are the Son of God, command these stones to become loaves of bread." ⁴But he answered, "It is written, 'One does not live by bread alone, but by every word that comes from the mouth of God.'" ⁵Then the devil took him to the holy city and placed him on the pinnacle of the temple, ⁶saying to him, "If you are the Son of God, throw yourself down; for it is written, 'He will command his angels concerning you,' and 'On their hands they will bear you up, so that you will not dash your foot against a stone.'" ⁷Jesus said to him, "Again it is written, 'Do not put the Lord your God to the test.'" ⁸Again, the devil took him to a very high mountain and showed him all the kingdoms of the world and their splendor; ⁹and he said to him, "All these I will give you, if you will fall down and worship me." ¹⁰Jesus said to him, "Away with you, Satan! for it is written, 'Worship the Lord your God, and serve only him.'" ¹¹Then the devil left him, and suddenly angels came and waited on him.

¹²Now when Jesus heard that John had been arrested, he withdrew to Galilee. ¹³He left Nazareth and made his home in Capernaum by the sea, in the territory of Zebulun and Naphtali, ¹⁴so that what had been spoken through the prophet Isaiah might be fulfilled: ¹⁵"Land of Zebulun, land of Naphtali, on the road

by the sea, across the Jordan, Galilee of the Gentiles—[16]the people who sat in darkness have seen a great light, and for those who sat in the region and shadow of death light has dawned." [17]From that time Jesus began to proclaim, "Repent, for the kingdom of heaven has come near."

[18]As he walked by the Sea of Galilee, he saw two brothers, Simon, who is called Peter, and Andrew his brother, casting a net into the sea—for they were fishermen. [19]And he said to them, "Follow me, and I will make you fish for people." [20]Immediately they left their nets and followed him. [21]As he went from there, he saw two other brothers, James son of Zebedee and his brother John, in the boat with their father Zebedee, mending their nets, and he called them. [22]Immediately they left the boat and their father, and followed him.

Reflection

Jesus begins his ministry in the Jordan River with the baptism by John. Immediately the Spirit leads him into the wilderness to fast for forty (!) days—Matthew's way of reminding us of Israel's forty years in the wilderness. During the forty days Jesus spends in the desert, he faces various temptations that could draw him away from his daring mission to save the human race from itself. The specific temptations have a common theme: they tempt Jesus to "play it safe" as a way of seeking to fulfill his mission of salvation.

Now, of course, playing it safe is a favorite choice of individuals and organizations. In theory, it's a low-risk, no-risk path ahead. Playing it safe avoids difficult choices, painful solutions…it's a fast and easy way ahead with none of the pain or peril. That's the great temptation Jesus was offered in the wilderness: to play it safe as a way of achieving the salvation of the human race.

I read somewhere that in India many years ago, a person who attended university and failed to graduate was given a card that read: "Bachelor of Arts attempted and failed." The card was given as an affirmation, not as a judgment, with the belief being that someone who attempted something and failed was of more value to society than someone who never risked failure.

Jesus chose not to yield to the temptation to play it safe, and in doing so faced the failure of the cross. Ultimately, God took that failure and, through the power of divine love, used it to win the salvation of the world. And your salvation and mine.

The Rt. Rev. Clifton Daniel
Bishop of the Diocese of Pennsylvania
Philadelphia, Pennsylvania

A Journey with Matthew

Questions

What might you be called to risk in order to realize a dream or attain a goal?

How might you be tempted to "play it safe?"

How might you help empower others to take risks in God's service?

Prayer

Almighty God, strengthen our resolve to serve others in your name. Free us from love of safety so that we might love boldly; free us from dedication to self to embrace service of others. Give us courage to live out your mission of justice and love, hope and forgiveness in this world broken and enslaved by sin. Use us to help free your church from its sedate ways, set it on fire with the power of your Spirit, and empower it to take bold risks to proclaim your love; through Jesus Christ our Lord, who was tempted in every way as we are and yet did not sin. Amen.

Matthew 4:23—5:20

23Jesus went throughout Galilee, teaching in their synagogues and proclaiming the good news of the kingdom and curing every disease and every sickness among the people. 24So his fame spread throughout all Syria, and they brought to him all the sick, those who were afflicted with various diseases and pains, demoniacs, epileptics, and paralytics, and he cured them. 25And great crowds followed him from Galilee, the Decapolis, Jerusalem, Judea, and from beyond the Jordan.

5 When Jesus saw the crowds, he went up the mountain; and after he sat down, his disciples came to him. 2Then he began to speak, and taught them, saying:

3"Blessed are the poor in spirit, for theirs is the kingdom of heaven.

4Blessed are those who mourn, for they will be comforted. 5Blessed are the meek, for they will inherit the earth. 6Blessed are those who hunger and thirst for righteousness, for they will be filled. 7Blessed are the merciful, for they will receive mercy. 8Blessed are the pure in heart, for they will see God. 9Blessed are the peacemakers, for they will be called children of God. 10Blessed are those who are persecuted for righteousness' sake, for theirs is the kingdom of heaven. 11Blessed are you when people revile you and persecute you and utter all kinds of evil against you falsely on my account. 12Rejoice and be glad, for your reward is great in heaven, for in the same way they persecuted the prophets who were before you.

[13]"You are the salt of the earth; but if salt has lost its taste, how can its saltiness be restored? It is no longer good for anything, but is thrown out and trampled under foot. [14]You are the light of the world. A city built on a hill cannot be hid. [15]No one after lighting a lamp puts it under the bushel basket, but on the lampstand, and it gives light to all in the house. [16]In the same way, let your light shine before others, so that they may see your good works and give glory to your Father in heaven.

[17]"Do not think that I have come to abolish the law or the prophets; I have come not to abolish but to fulfill. [18]For truly I tell you, until heaven and earth pass away, not one letter, not one stroke of a letter, will pass from the law until all is accomplished. [19]Therefore, whoever breaks one of the least of these commandments, and teaches others to do the same, will be called least in the kingdom of heaven; but whoever does them and teaches them will be called great in the kingdom of heaven. [20]For I tell you, unless your righteousness exceeds that of the scribes and Pharisees, you will never enter the kingdom of heaven."

Reflection

This passage brings us to the Sermon on the Mount. I think many of us read all of these "blessed" statements as comforting, as if they are meant to make us feel better. However, the last couple of beatitudes should be read as challenges for most of us. At least in the developed world, most of us Christians will never personally know persecution, and for this, we should give thanks.

However, I think the gospel is suggesting that if we are really following Jesus—if we fully accept his invitation to be faithful—our very lives will be both witnesses to Jesus and challenges to the world. When we "proclaim the good news of the kingdom", we are subverting the empire of our time. Much of our culture will prefer shadows and will not appreciate the "light of the world." Following Jesus is extraordinarily difficult, demanding righteousness greater even than the scribes and Pharisees. I haven't heard very many sermons about this aspect of the Christian life—trying harder than the Pharisees!

Perhaps we do well to read the Sermon on the Mount as a challenge, not as a sentimental, greeting-card-worthy collection of sayings. If we are really following Jesus, we will get ourselves into trouble. Matthew assures us here that even then, Christ will be a blessing to us.

The Rev. Scott Gunn
Executive Director of Forward Movement
Cincinnati, Ohio

A Journey with Matthew

Questions

Do you agree that following Jesus may get us into trouble? Have you ever experienced this or known someone who has? Was it a blessing?

Why did so many people embrace Jesus' call to follow him, given his dire warning?

Prayer

Lord Jesus Christ, give us courage and strength to follow you where we are called to go, not just where it is easy. Amen.

Matthew 5:21-48

[21]"You have heard that it was said to those of ancient times, 'You shall not murder'; and 'whoever murders shall be liable to judgment.' [22]But I say to you that if you are angry with a brother or sister, you will be liable to judgment; and if you insult a brother or sister, you will be liable to the council; and if you say, 'You fool,' you will be liable to the hell of fire. [23]So when you are offering your gift at the altar, if you remember that your brother or sister has something against you, [24]leave your gift there before the altar and go; first be reconciled to your brother or sister, and then come and offer your gift. [25]Come to terms quickly with your accuser while you are on the way to court with him, or your accuser may hand you over to the judge, and the judge to the guard, and you will be thrown into prison. [26]Truly I tell you, you will never get out until you have paid the last penny.

[27]"You have heard that it was said, 'You shall not commit adultery.' [28]But I say to you that everyone who looks at a woman with lust has already committed adultery with her in his heart. [29]If your right eye causes you to sin, tear it out and throw it away; it is better for you to lose one of your members than for your whole body to be thrown into hell. [30]And if your right hand causes you to sin, cut it off and throw it away; it is better for you to lose one of your members than for your whole body to go into hell. [31]It was also said, 'Whoever divorces his wife, let him give her a certificate of divorce.' [32]But I say to you that anyone who divorces his wife, except on the ground of unchastity,

causes her to commit adultery; and whoever marries a divorced woman commits adultery.

[33]"Again, you have heard that it was said to those of ancient times, 'You shall not swear falsely, but carry out the vows you have made to the Lord.' [34]But I say to you, Do not swear at all, either by heaven, for it is the throne of God, [35]or by the earth, for it is his footstool, or by Jerusalem, for it is the city of the great King. [36]And do not swear by your head, for you cannot make one hair white or black. [37]Let your word be 'Yes, Yes' or 'No, No'; anything more than this comes from the evil one.

[38]"You have heard that it was said, 'An eye for an eye and a tooth for a tooth.' [39]But I say to you, Do not resist an evildoer. But if anyone strikes you on the right cheek, turn the other also; [40]and if anyone wants to sue you and take your coat, give your cloak as well; [41]and if anyone forces you to go one mile, go also the second mile. [42]Give to everyone who begs from you, and do not refuse anyone who wants to borrow from you.

[43]"You have heard that it was said, 'You shall love your neighbor and hate your enemy.' [44]But I say to you, Love your enemies and pray for those who persecute you, [45]so that you may be children of your Father in heaven; for he makes his sun rise on the evil and on the good, and sends rain on the righteous and on the unrighteous. [46]For if you love those who love you, what reward do you have? Do not even the tax collectors do the same? [47]And if you greet only your brothers and sisters, what more are you doing than others? Do not even the Gentiles do the same? [48]Be perfect, therefore, as your heavenly Father is perfect."

Reflection

Jesus here continues his challenging teaching, reminding his followers—and us—that it is not enough to fulfill the letter of the law. Rather, what is in our heart matters as much as what we do.

I am certainly well acquainted with anger, and Jesus' teaching that my anger makes me "liable to judgment" is hard to hear. Of course, there is great wisdom here. Anger consumes the heart, and when rage is kindled within me, I am not able to be my best self, to love others, or even to love God fully. This is why reconciliation is so very important.

Then we come to the tough bits about retaliation and loving our enemies. How different would our world be if we sincerely and devoutly prayed for our enemies, if we loved them, rather than wishing our enemies harm or dispatching armies to kill them? I'm not sure how this plays out in foreign policy, but I do know that every time I have prayed for the well-being of someone who has harmed me, my heart has been transformed. It is not easy to hear, but the call of the gospel is not "they should be punished as they deserve" but rather that we should love our enemies. We are called to be perfect, something that we will never achieve, though the quest will bring us ever closer to Jesus.

The Rev. Scott Gunn
Executive Director of Forward Movement
Cincinnati, Ohio

A Journey with Matthew

Questions_____

Taking one example, Jesus says to "Give to everyone who begs from you." This command must have presented some of the same challenges to Jesus' listeners as it does to us today. Why do you think Jesus asks this of his followers?

For several days, try praying for an enemy, perhaps a coworker or a relative or a terrorist. Does this change you? Do you think it changes your enemy?

Prayer _____

What you ask of us is impossible, Lord Jesus, and so we beg you to help us repent and try again whenever we fail to follow you. Amen.

Matthew 6:1-18

6"Beware of practicing your piety before others in order to be seen by them; for then you have no reward from your Father in heaven. ²So whenever you give alms, do not sound a trumpet before you, as the hypocrites do in the synagogues and in the streets, so that they may be praised by others. Truly I tell you, they have received their reward. ³But when you give alms, do not let your left hand know what your right hand is doing, ⁴so that your alms may be done in secret; and your Father who sees in secret will reward you.

⁵"And whenever you pray, do not be like the hypocrites; for they love to stand and pray in the synagogues and at the street corners, so that they may be seen by others. Truly I tell you, they have received their reward.

⁶But whenever you pray, go into your room and shut the door and pray to your Father who is in secret; and your Father who sees in secret will reward you. ⁷When you are praying, do not heap up empty phrases as the Gentiles do; for they think that they will be heard because of their many words. ⁸Do not be like them, for your Father knows what you need before you ask him.

⁹"Pray then in this way: Our Father in heaven, hallowed be your name. ¹⁰Your kingdom come. Your will be done, on earth as it is in heaven. ¹¹Give us this day our daily bread. ¹²And forgive us our debts, as we also have forgiven our debtors. ¹³And do not bring us to the time of trial, but rescue us from the evil one. ¹⁴For if you forgive others their trespasses, your

heavenly Father will also forgive you; [15]but if you do not forgive others, neither will your Father forgive your trespasses.

[16]"And whenever you fast, do not look dismal, like the hypocrites, for they disfigure their faces so as to show others that they are fasting. Truly I tell you, they have received their reward. [17]But when you fast, put oil on your head and wash your face, [18]so that your fasting may be seen not by others but by your Father who is in secret; and your Father who sees in secret will reward you."

Reflection

The Lord's Prayer is the prayer Jesus taught his disciples, and it is both simple and comprehensive because it has every element a prayer should contain. It reminds us that God is the father of all people and therefore we, as God's children, are automatically related to one another as well. It is not possible to have a relationship with God that excludes others. Addressed as father, the image at best is one of God's closeness toward us.

The three first petitions ask that we might live as people who in turn put our trust in God and seek to live by God's values toward our brothers and sisters. These are the values exemplified by Jesus—love, joy, justice, compassion, mercy, and forgiveness. It asks that we might live as God intends us to live, human beings loved by God who in turn try to love others made in God's image.

The second part of the prayer asks God for the things we need to live out the commitment we have made in the first part. Bread stands for everything that sustains us so that we can live by God's values. We ask for an appreciation of the depth of God's forgiveness so that we in turn might forgive others, and for God's help at those critical moments when we might be tempted to live simply for ourselves and ignore the world and its needs. It is a prayer that God's priorities for humanity might become ours.

The Most Rev. Barry Morgan
Archbishop of Wales
Cardiff, Wales

Questions

Do you find it easy to address God as father?

Which part of the Lord's Prayer do you find the most difficult to live out?

Prayer

Lord God, enable us to not only pray the words of Jesus but also to live them out as his followers. Amen.

Matthew 6:19-34

19"Do not store up for yourselves treasures on earth, where moth and rust consume and where thieves break in and steal; 20but store up for yourselves treasures in heaven, where neither moth nor rust consumes and where thieves do not break in and steal. 21For where your treasure is, there your heart will be also. 22The eye is the lamp of the body. So, if your eye is healthy, your whole body will be full of light; 23but if your eye is unhealthy, your whole body will be full of darkness. If then the light in you is darkness, how great is the darkness! 24No one can serve two masters; for a slave will either hate the one and love the other, or be devoted to the one and despise the other. You cannot serve God and wealth.

25"Therefore I tell you, do not worry about your life, what you will eat or what you will drink, or about your body, what you will wear. Is not life more than food, and the body more than clothing? 26Look at the birds of the air; they neither sow nor reap nor gather into barns, and yet your heavenly Father feeds them. Are you not of more value than they? 27And can any of you by worrying add a single hour to your span of life? 28And why do you worry about clothing? Consider the lilies of the field, how they grow; they neither toil nor spin, 29yet I tell you, even Solomon in all his glory was not clothed like one of these. 30But if God so clothes the grass of the field, which is alive today and tomorrow is thrown into the oven, will he not much more clothe you—you of little faith? 31Therefore do not worry, saying, 'What will we eat?' or 'What will we drink?' or

'What will we wear?' ³²For it is the Gentiles who strive for all these things; and indeed your heavenly Father knows that you need all these things. ³³But strive first for the kingdom of God and his righteousness, and all these things will be given to you as well. ³⁴"So do not worry about tomorrow, for tomorrow will bring worries of its own. Today's trouble is enough for today."

Reflection

If we lived by the values of the gospel as outlined in the Lord's Prayer, our trust in God would be so complete that we would not worry about our daily sustenance. Yet we tend not to live like that—we worry about tomorrow and the future, both for ourselves and for our children. We make plans for that future, both short- and long-term, in all kinds of ways. Yet did not Jesus in the parable of the talents blame the person who simply buried his talent in the ground for not thinking ahead of how he might use it?

Perhaps what Jesus is warning us against in this section of the Sermon on the Mount is not so much prudent planning for the future but a total preoccupation with it— worrying about it to such an extent that it takes over our lives, which is ultimately a failure to trust in God. The man who built bigger barns for his crops is condemned, not so much for providing for the future, but for being so taken up with it that he could think of nothing else. Over-anxiety and preoccupation about the future is something that hinders the coming of God's rule and kingdom because in the end, it is centered on self and not on God.

The Most Rev. Barry Morgan
Archbishop of Wales
Cardiff, Wales

Questions

Do you think that it is preoccupation with rather than prudence about planning for the future that is the thrust of Jesus' message?

When has prudence given way to preoccupation in your life? How might you find balance?

Prayer

Lord, help us to entrust ourselves, all that we have and all that we are, to your service. And, we pray, free us from anxiety. Amen.

Matthew 7:1-20

7 "Do not judge, so that you may not be judged. ²For with the judgment you make you will be judged, and the measure you give will be the measure you get. ³Why do you see the speck in your neighbor's eye, but do not notice the log in your own eye? ⁴Or how can you say to your neighbor, 'Let me take the speck out of your eye,' while the log is in your own eye? ⁵You hypocrite, first take the log out of your own eye, and then you will see clearly to take the speck out of your neighbor's eye. ⁶Do not give what is holy to dogs; and do not throw your pearls before swine, or they will trample them under foot and turn and maul you.

⁷"Ask, and it will be given you; search, and you will find; knock, and the door will be opened for you. ⁸For everyone who asks receives, and everyone who searches finds, and for everyone who knocks, the door will be opened. ⁹Is there anyone among you who, if your child asks for bread, will give a stone? ¹⁰Or if the child asks for a fish, will give a snake? ¹¹If you then, who are evil, know how to give good gifts to your children, how much more will your Father in heaven give good things to those who ask him!

¹²"In everything do to others as you would have them do to you; for this is the law and the prophets. ¹³"Enter through the narrow gate; for the gate is wide and the road is easy that leads to destruction, and there are many who take it. ¹⁴For the gate is narrow and the road is hard that leads to life, and there are few who find it.

[15]"Beware of false prophets, who come to you in sheep's clothing but inwardly are ravenous wolves. [16]You will know them by their fruits. Are grapes gathered from thorns, or figs from thistles? [17]In the same way, every good tree bears good fruit, but the bad tree bears bad fruit. [18]A good tree cannot bear bad fruit, nor can a bad tree bear good fruit. [19]Every tree that does not bear good fruit is cut down and thrown into the fire. [20]Thus you will know them by their fruits."

Reflection

Chapter seven of Matthew's Gospel continues in the style of the Beatitudes in chapter five. Examining the whole—a collection of fragments scattered over a range of issues and behaviors—may be of greater value than any single component. The temptation to drill into a specific verse or teaching can distract from the role these chapters play in Matthew's account.

The Sermon on the Mount, the setting of the Beatitudes, may or may not have been an historical event. What's important about it is that the author found this device a useful way of framing an extensive collection of Jesus' teachings. By the time we reach chapter seven, the teachings themselves read somewhat like morals in search of fables—or teachings in search of parables. Taken individually, more than one of the verses in chapter seven sounds like the concluding sentence of a longer story.

It's as though the author polled a gathering of Jesus' followers, asking, "What teaching of Jesus do you recall?" and dutifully recorded their spontaneous replies. In a community accustomed to the oral transmission of story and information, the distilled learning from Jesus' discourses would have been the salient summary, the lasting takeaway. The end result bears a resemblance to Hebrew wisdom literature like the Book of Proverbs, likely intentionally. Interestingly, the succeeding passage (7:24-27) concludes the long catalog of fragmented sayings with the illustration comparing foundations of sand and rock, the latter being the basis for wisdom.

The Rev. Sam Portaro
Author and Retreat Leader
Chicago, Illinois

Questions

Taking some or all of the separate teachings in this passage, what story from your own life might you tell to illustrate each?

Recall one or more of the foundational principles that guide your life and actions. How might you briefly summarize the principle, and can you recall—and retell—the longer story of how you learned and appropriated the principle?

Prayer

God, grant us the grace and patience to reflect upon our daily experiences that we might discern and distill the wisdom to be gleaned therein. Amen.

Matthew 7:21—8:13

[21]"Not everyone who says to me, 'Lord, Lord,' will enter the kingdom of heaven, but only the one who does the will of my Father in heaven. [22]On that day many will say to me, 'Lord, Lord, did we not prophesy in your name, and cast out demons in your name, and do many deeds of power in your name?' [23]Then I will declare to them, 'I never knew you; go away from me, you evildoers.' [24]"Everyone then who hears these words of mine and acts on them will be like a wise man who built his house on rock. [25]The rain fell, the floods came, and the winds blew and beat on that house, but it did not fall, because it had been founded on rock. [26]And everyone who hears these words of mine and does not act on them will be like a foolish man who built his house on sand. [27]The rain fell, and the floods came, and the winds blew and beat against that house, and it fell—and great was its fall!" [28]Now when Jesus had finished saying these things, the crowds were astounded at his teaching, [29]for he taught them as one having authority, and not as their scribes.

8 When Jesus had come down from the mountain, great crowds followed him; [2]and there was a leper who came to him and knelt before him, saying, "Lord, if you choose, you can make me clean." [3]He stretched out his hand and touched him, saying, "I do choose. Be made clean!" Immediately his leprosy was cleansed. [4]Then Jesus said to him, "See that you say nothing to anyone; but go, show yourself to the priest, and offer the gift that Moses commanded, as a testimony to them."

⁵When he entered Capernaum, a centurion came to him, appealing to him ⁶and saying, "Lord, my servant is lying at home paralyzed, in terrible distress." ⁷And he said to him, "I will come and cure him." ⁸The centurion answered, "Lord, I am not worthy to have you come under my roof; but only speak the word, and my servant will be healed. ⁹For I also am a man under authority, with soldiers under me; and I say to one, 'Go,' and he goes, and to another, 'Come,' and he comes, and to my slave, 'Do this,' and the slave does it." ¹⁰When Jesus heard him, he was amazed and said to those who followed him, "Truly I tell you, in no one in Israel have I found such faith. ¹¹I tell you, many will come from east and west and will eat with Abraham and Isaac and Jacob in the kingdom of heaven, ¹²while the heirs of the kingdom will be thrown into the outer darkness, where there will be weeping and gnashing of teeth." ¹³And to the centurion Jesus said, "Go; let it be done for you according to your faith." And the servant was healed in that hour.

Reflection

The pivotal word in this portion of the Gospel of Matthew is authority (7:29). Ascribed to Jesus by his hearers and cited as the criterion upon which their trust is based, Jesus' authority is differentiated from the authority claimed by the scribes, whose teachings fall under the category "don't do as I do, do as I say," a difference essential to discerning false prophets from true ones in the fruit of actions (7:15-20).

What emerges is the value of personal experience as a compelling source of authority. Most of us form our judgments of truth by consonance with life experience. For example, when Jesus says "the measure you give will be the measure you get," (7:2) my own story verifies the stated truth with personal experience. Those who compare the lessons of chapters five through seven with their own experience likely had little difficulty discerning its wisdom.

Thus, when we come to the story of two healings in chapter eight, it's not the cures but the characters who are central: the leper and the centurion—and a corollary of authority: trust and faith. The leper declares confidence in Jesus upfront; the centurion confesses his faith with an allusion to authority.

Moreover, there's a subtle movement from the leper whose faith in Jesus is met with healing, to the centurion whose servant is healed in absentia by Jesus, who says, "let it be done for you according to your faith" (8:13). The leper is healed by Jesus' own hand, whereas the centurion's servant is healed through the centurion himself in a foreshadowing of authority that will be granted to disciples themselves (Matthew 10).

This progression points to Jesus' encouragement that his followers trust in their own authority, derived from faith in God's truth as revealed in their own lives. This is the basis of the Roman Catholic appeal to individual conscience as the final arbiter of action, the Protestant assurance in the ultimate authority of trust in God's grace, and the admonition by Paul to "work out (one's) own salvation in fear and trembling" (Philippians 2:12) This "fear and trembling" is the humble human response to any undertaking of trust with dangerous consequences, the only antidote to which is a reliance built upon the foundation of a relationship with God.

The Rev. Sam Portaro
Author and Retreat Leader
Chicago, Illinois

Questions

Can you identify examples from your own experience when you moved from skepticism to trust based on personal experience?

When have you been moved by personal experience to decisive action or a principled stand in conflict with established social, political, or religious practice?

Prayer

God, grant us strength to rely upon your encouragement, and to trust in your love and grace revealed in our own lives, relationships, and experience. Amen.

Matthew 8:14-34

¹⁴When Jesus entered Peter's house, he saw his mother-in-law lying in bed with a fever; ¹⁵he touched her hand, and the fever left her, and she got up and began to serve him. ¹⁶That evening they brought to him many who were possessed with demons; and he cast out the spirits with a word, and cured all who were sick. ¹⁷This was to fulfill what had been spoken through the prophet Isaiah, "He took our infirmities and bore our diseases."

¹⁸Now when Jesus saw great crowds around him, he gave orders to go over to the other side. ¹⁹A scribe then approached and said, "Teacher, I will follow you wherever you go." ²⁰And Jesus said to him, "Foxes have holes, and birds of the air have nests; but the Son of Man has nowhere to lay his head."

²¹Another of his disciples said to him, "Lord, first let me go and bury my father." ²²But Jesus said to him, "Follow me, and let the dead bury their own dead."

²³And when he got into the boat, his disciples followed him. ²⁴A windstorm arose on the sea, so great that the boat was being swamped by the waves; but he was asleep. ²⁵And they went and woke him up, saying, "Lord, save us! We are perishing!" ²⁶And he said to them, "Why are you afraid, you of little faith?" Then he got up and rebuked the winds and the sea; and there was a dead calm. ²⁷They were amazed, saying, "What sort of man is this, that even the winds and the sea obey him?"

²⁸When he came to the other side, to the country of the Gadarenes, two demoniacs coming out of the tombs met

him. They were so fierce that no one could pass that way. [29]Suddenly they shouted, "What have you to do with us, Son of God? Have you come here to torment us before the time?" [30]Now a large herd of swine was feeding at some distance from them. [31]The demons begged him, "If you cast us out, send us into the herd of swine." [32]And he said to them, "Go!" So they came out and entered the swine; and suddenly, the whole herd rushed down the steep bank into the sea and perished in the water. [33]The swineherds ran off, and on going into the town, they told the whole story about what had happened to the demoniacs. [34]Then the whole town came out to meet Jesus; and when they saw him, they begged him to leave their neighborhood.

Reflection

Jesus was sleeping through a storm. How exhausted he must have been! And he was so relaxed that he didn't even awaken when the waves crashed into the boat. He almost sounded grumpy when the disciples woke him. "Why are you scared?" he asked. Jesus was not afraid.

That seems to be one of the major distinctions between God and humanity. God is not afraid, and we are. When angels visit people all throughout scripture, they usually begin by saying, "Don't be afraid!" Why are we so afraid? And why is God not afraid?

My youngest son often wakes in the middle of the night and calls for me. When I ask him why he is afraid, he cannot articulate why. He is just afraid of the dark, of the unknown, and of being alone. Simply my presence in his room often helps.

Humans have limited vision. We cannot see the future. We know that we all must die at some point, but none of us knows when. Our limited vision causes us to feel fear. We gaze into the dark, into the unknown, and feel fear. But God sees all, past and present and future. And for God, there is no fear, for nothing is unknown, nothing is uncertain.

Jesus says that those who are afraid are those of "little faith." So for Jesus, the antidote to fear is faith, trust in the love and benevolence of God. In other words, if we believe in the resurrection, we will not be afraid of dying, and when we are not afraid of dying, what else is there to fear?

Jesus calms the storms of our lives as he calmed the storm at sea. When we are afraid, all we need to do is call for him, as my son calls for me. When Jesus enters our lives and reminds us of his presence and we realize that we are not alone, something shifts, and the darkness is not so dark anymore. We will never be able to see the future, not in this life, but we can trust in the One who does.

The Very Rev. Kate Morehead
Dean of St. John's Cathedral
Jacksonville, Florida

Questions

What are you afraid of? Sit quietly and identify your fears. What would it feel like if you invited Jesus to experience them with you?

Prayer

Lord Jesus, calm our fears as you calmed the storm at sea. Help us to trust that you alone can see past, present, and future, and that if you are not afraid, then we need not be afraid. Give us faith in your eternal changelessness. Amen.

Matthew 9:1-26

9And after getting into a boat he crossed the sea and came to his own town. [2]And just then some people were carrying a paralyzed man lying on a bed. When Jesus saw their faith, he said to the paralytic, "Take heart, son; your sins are forgiven." [3]Then some of the scribes said to themselves, "This man is blaspheming." [4]But Jesus, perceiving their thoughts, said, "Why do you think evil in your hearts? [5]For which is easier, to say, 'Your sins are forgiven,' or to say, 'Stand up and walk'? [6]But so that you may know that the Son of Man has authority on earth to forgive sins" —he then said to the paralytic— "stand up, take your bed and go to your home." [7]And he stood up and went to his home. [8]When the crowds saw it, they were filled with awe, and they glorified God, who had given such authority to human beings.

[9]As Jesus was walking along, he saw a man called Matthew sitting at the tax booth; and he said to him, "Follow me." And he got up and followed him. [10]And as he sat at dinner in the house, many tax collectors and sinners came and were sitting with him and his disciples. [11]When the Pharisees saw this, they said to his disciples, "Why does your teacher eat with tax collectors and sinners?" [12]But when he heard this, he said, "Those who are well have no need of a physician, but those who are sick. [13]Go and learn what this means, 'I desire mercy, not sacrifice.' For I have come to call not the righteous but sinners."

[14]Then the disciples of John came to him, saying, "Why do

we and the Pharisees fast often, but your disciples do not fast?" ¹⁵And Jesus said to them, "The wedding guests cannot mourn as long as the bridegroom is with them, can they? The days will come when the bridegroom is taken away from them, and then they will fast. ¹⁶No one sews a piece of unshrunk cloth on an old cloak, for the patch pulls away from the cloak, and a worse tear is made. ¹⁷Neither is new wine put into old wineskins; otherwise, the skins burst, and the wine is spilled, and the skins are destroyed; but new wine is put into fresh wineskins, and so both are preserved."

¹⁸While he was saying these things to them, suddenly a leader of the synagogue came in and knelt before him, saying, "My daughter has just died; but come and lay your hand on her, and she will live." ¹⁹And Jesus got up and followed him, with his disciples. ²⁰Then suddenly a woman who had been suffering from hemorrhages for twelve years came up behind him and touched the fringe of his cloak, ²¹for she said to herself, "If I only touch his cloak, I will be made well." ²²Jesus turned, and seeing her he said, "Take heart, daughter; your faith has made you well." And instantly the woman was made well. ²³When Jesus came to the leader's house and saw the flute players and the crowd making a commotion, ²⁴he said, "Go away; for the girl is not dead but sleeping." And they laughed at him. ²⁵But when the crowd had been put outside, he went in and took her by the hand, and the girl got up. ²⁶And the report of this spread throughout that district.

Reflection

Why did Jesus choose a tax collector as his disciple? Tax collectors were the IRS agents of their day. They were often heartless and would try to collect taxes from the poorest of the poor. They worked for a government that was wealthy and unjust. They were willing to hurt the poor in order to make the rich richer. Why choose a tax collector?

The only answer I have is that Jesus looked at the inside of a person. Jesus must have seen much more in Matthew than just a tax collector. When Jesus looked at this Jewish extortioner, he saw what Matthew would become, the author of a gospel, a devout follower of Christ. Jesus saw the potential of the man and not just his external trappings.

What if we were to look upon others with an eye for their internal potential rather than just an external evaluation? What if we sought out and believed in those who did not look so good on the outside but had enormous potential on the inside? Can that even be done?

Saint Paul says that our hearts have eyes: "with the eyes of your heart enlightened…" (Ephesians 1:18). Love can impact the way we perceive other people. Love can cause us to look again.

Most people would have walked right by Matthew with disgust, but Jesus saw something more than a tax collector. He saw a disciple. And in seeing Matthew as a disciple, Jesus could invite him to be one. How can we change the lives of those around us simply by seeing them differently?

The Very Rev. Kate Morehead
Dean of St. John's Cathedral
Jacksonville, Florida

Questions

Who have you judged in your life? Can you take a moment and try to see that person with the eyes of your heart? Is there goodness within him or her? If so, how can you call that goodness forth?

Prayer

Lord Jesus, help us to look upon others not with harsh judgment but with the eyes of our heart enlightened. Help us to look not just at outward trappings but into the soul of a person. Help us to see potential in others and to call forth goodness. Amen.

Matthew 9:27—10:15

27As Jesus went on from there, two blind men followed him, crying loudly, "Have mercy on us, Son of David!" 28When he entered the house, the blind men came to him; and Jesus said to them, "Do you believe that I am able to do this?" They said to him, "Yes, Lord." 29Then he touched their eyes and said, "According to your faith let it be done to you." 30And their eyes were opened. Then Jesus sternly ordered them, "See that no one knows of this." 31But they went away and spread the news about him throughout that district. 32After they had gone away, a demoniac who was mute was brought to him. 33And when the demon had been cast out, the one who had been mute spoke; and the crowds were amazed and said, "Never has anything like this been seen in Israel."

34But the Pharisees said, "By the ruler of the demons he casts out the demons."

35Then Jesus went about all the cities and villages, teaching in their synagogues, and proclaiming the good news of the kingdom, and curing every disease and every sickness. 36When he saw the crowds, he had compassion for them, because they were harassed and helpless, like sheep without a shepherd. 37Then he said to his disciples, "The harvest is plentiful, but the laborers are few; 38therefore ask the Lord of the harvest to send out laborers into his harvest."

10 Then Jesus summoned his twelve disciples and gave them authority over unclean spirits, to cast them out, and to cure every disease and every sickness. 2These are the names

of the twelve apostles: first, Simon, also known as Peter, and his brother Andrew; James son of Zebedee, and his brother John; ³Philip and Bartholomew; Thomas and Matthew the tax collector; James son of Alphaeus, and Thaddaeus; ⁴Simon the Cananaean, and Judas Iscariot, the one who betrayed him.

⁵These twelve Jesus sent out with the following instructions: "Go nowhere among the Gentiles, and enter no town of the Samaritans, ⁶but go rather to the lost sheep of the house of Israel. ⁷As you go, proclaim the good news, 'The kingdom of heaven has come near.' ⁸Cure the sick, raise the dead, cleanse the lepers, cast out demons. You received without payment; give without payment. ⁹Take no gold, or silver, or copper in your belts, ¹⁰no bag for your journey, or two tunics, or sandals, or a staff; for laborers deserve their food. ¹¹Whatever town or village you enter, find out who in it is worthy, and stay there until you leave. ¹²As you enter the house, greet it. ¹³If the house is worthy, let your peace come upon it; but if it is not worthy, let your peace return to you. ¹⁴If anyone will not welcome you or listen to your words, shake off the dust from your feet as you leave that house or town. ¹⁵Truly I tell you, it will be more tolerable for the land of Sodom and Gomorrah on the day of judgment than for that town."

Reflection

Do you believe? The story of the blind men seeing Jesus and recognizing something extraordinary about him reminds me of a phenomenon that takes place in recovery circles. People affected by addictions (sometimes blinded, figuratively) see others who have overcome battles with addiction and are now happy, joyous, and free.

Sometimes, having tried and still fallen back so many times, people don't believe they can ever "get it," and recovery from addiction seems to be something that happens to other people and not them. There is good reason for this: Addiction is a progressive disease and those who find themselves returning to it again and again often find themselves in a darker, lower, scarier place than the previous bottom. It is no surprise to hear them say they no longer believe they can do it.

In today's reading, Jesus asks the two blind men if they believe he is able to do this, to restore them to sight. In a similar vein, often those who are attempting to guide people out of their addictions, toward the light, tell them they don't have to believe that they can get clean and sober. Rather they just have to believe that someone else believes they can do it.

Sometimes, we have to believe for others.

Bo Cox
Author and Counselor
Norman, Oklahoma

Questions_____

Have you ever been inspired by another person to do something you thought wasn't possible?

Assuming you've overcome some shortcomings in your life, can you see how those victories can be beacons of hope for people still struggling with their own battles?

Prayer _____

God, creator of us all, help to create in us open hearts that realize our need for miracles. Help us accept that miracles often come in the form of our fellow travelers. And help us to remember that we, too, may be someone's miracle. Amen.

Matthew 10:16-42

[16]"See, I am sending you out like sheep into the midst of wolves; so be wise as serpents and innocent as doves. [17]Beware of them, for they will hand you over to councils and flog you in their synagogues; [18]and you will be dragged before governors and kings because of me, as a testimony to them and the Gentiles. [19]When they hand you over, do not worry about how you are to speak or what you are to say; for what you are to say will be given to you at that time; [20]for it is not you who speak, but the Spirit of your Father speaking through you. [21]Brother will betray brother to death, and a father his child, and children will rise against parents and have them put to death; [22]and you will be hated by all because of my name. But the one who endures to the end will be saved. [23]When they persecute you in one town, flee to the next; for truly I tell you, you will not have gone through all the towns of Israel before the Son of Man comes. [24]A disciple is not above the teacher, nor a slave above the master; [25]it is enough for the disciple to be like the teacher, and the slave like the master. If they have called the master of the house Beelzebul, how much more will they malign those of his household! [26]So have no fear of them; for nothing is covered up that will not be uncovered, and nothing secret that will not become known. [27]What I say to you in the dark, tell in the light; and what you hear whispered, proclaim from the housetops. [28]Do not fear those who kill the body but cannot kill the soul; rather fear him who can destroy both soul and body in hell. [29]Are not two sparrows sold for a penny? Yet not one of them

will fall to the ground apart from your Father. ³⁰And even the hairs of your head are all counted. ³¹So do not be afraid; you are of more value than many sparrows. ³²"Everyone therefore who acknowledges me before others, I also will acknowledge before my Father in heaven; ³³but whoever denies me before others, I also will deny before my Father in heaven. ³⁴Do not think that I have come to bring peace to the earth; I have not come to bring peace, but a sword. ³⁵For I have come to set a man against his father, and a daughter against her mother, and a daughter-in-law against her mother-in-law; ³⁶and one's foes will be members of one's own household. ³⁷Whoever loves father or mother more than me is not worthy of me; and whoever loves son or daughter more than me is not worthy of me; ³⁸and whoever does not take up the cross and follow me is not worthy of me. ³⁹Those who find their life will lose it, and those who lose their life for my sake will find it. ⁴⁰"Whoever welcomes you welcomes me, and whoever welcomes me welcomes the one who sent me. ⁴¹Whoever welcomes a prophet in the name of a prophet will receive a prophet's reward; and whoever welcomes a righteous person in the name of a righteous person will receive the reward of the righteous; ⁴²and whoever gives even a cup of cold water to one of these little ones in the name of a disciple—truly I tell you, none of these will lose their reward."

Reflection

In this collection of writings about Jesus, people suddenly discover they have power in Jesus' name. Great things are possible. Suddenly the conversation turns divisive; floggings and family betrayal dominate the discourse.

It is human nature for us, when we have epiphanies, to want to share the good news with everyone we know. Think about the latest good recipe, good restaurant, or good movie; didn't you tell someone else the good news? If you have ever overcome a life challenge, doesn't the solution that worked for you become the solution you automatically offer to another when you see them struggle with a similar trial?

Power can be corruptive. People are human, and humans are fallible. When we combine our myopic tendency with power, it turns dangerous. History is rife with examples of powerful people who think they are right yet commit atrocities in the name of progress, destiny, and God.

Jesus turned the organized religion of his day on its ear. Inclusive in a system of exclusion, he brought love. In these writings he first touched people who were untouchable and later beseeched people to do his bidding for free. Love always trumps power.

Bo Cox
Author and Counselor
Norman, Oklahoma

Questions

When you think you have the right way, do you tend to become inflexible and condemning of others who don't share your view?

When you are at odds with another, do you find yourself wanting to be right or to get along?

Prayer

Creator of all that has been and ever shall be, as we seek to proclaim the Good News, fill us with compassion, tolerance, and acceptance of people and situations with which we may not agree or understand. Help us to closely follow the example of Christ who, rather than imposing his will, gave his life to spread his message. Amen.

Matthew 11:1-24

11 Now when Jesus had finished instructing his twelve disciples, he went on from there to teach and proclaim his message in their cities. ²When John heard in prison what the Messiah was doing, he sent word by his disciples ³and said to him, "Are you the one who is to come, or are we to wait for another?" ⁴Jesus answered them, "Go and tell John what you hear and see: ⁵the blind receive their sight, the lame walk, the lepers are cleansed, the deaf hear, the dead are raised, and the poor have good news brought to them. ⁶And blessed is anyone who takes no offense at me."

⁷As they went away, Jesus began to speak to the crowds about John: "What did you go out into the wilderness to look at? A reed shaken by the wind? ⁸What then did you go out to see? Someone dressed in soft robes? Look, those who wear soft robes are in royal palaces. ⁹What then did you go out to see? A prophet? Yes, I tell you, and more than a prophet. ¹⁰This is the one about whom it is written, 'See, I am sending my messenger ahead of you, who will prepare your way before you.' ¹¹Truly I tell you, among those born of women no one has arisen greater than John the Baptist; yet the least in the kingdom of heaven is greater than he. ¹²From the days of John the Baptist until now the kingdom of heaven has suffered violence, and the violent take it by force. ¹³For all the prophets and the law prophesied until John came; ¹⁴and if you are willing to accept it, he is Elijah who is to come. ¹⁵Let anyone with ears listen!

16"But to what will I compare this generation? It is like children sitting in the marketplaces and calling to one another, 17'We played the flute for you, and you did not dance; we wailed, and you did not mourn.' 18For John came neither eating nor drinking, and they say, 'He has a demon'; 19the Son of Man came eating and drinking, and they say, 'Look, a glutton and a drunkard, a friend of tax collectors and sinners!' Yet wisdom is vindicated by her deeds." 20Then he began to reproach the cities in which most of his deeds of power had been done, because they did not repent. 21"Woe to you, Chorazin! Woe to you, Bethsaida! For if the deeds of power done in you had been done in Tyre and Sidon, they would have repented long ago in sackcloth and ashes. 22But I tell you, on the day of judgment it will be more tolerable for Tyre and Sidon than for you. 23And you, Capernaum, will you be exalted to heaven? No, you will be brought down to Hades. For if the deeds of power done in you had been done in Sodom, it would have remained until this day. 24But I tell you that on the day of judgment it will be more tolerable for the land of Sodom than for you."

Reflection

I once visited the bedside of a sixty-seven-year-old woman, with her two grace-filled adult children by her side. They asked what they should know about dying. The son said he believed in God. But, he wasn't sure if Jesus was the way. The daughter had chosen to take the leap of faith and trust in Jesus Christ. The mother, dying of cancer, confessed that she was not a Christian. She wasn't sure what would happen when she died.

The gospel writer tells us of varying responses to Jesus. Some doubt and wonder and eventually choose to reject the Savior. Even John the Baptist, after all he has done to announce Jesus' coming, is puzzled, asks from his prison cell if we should look for someone else. Townspeople of Chorazin, Bethsaida, and Capernaum refuse to turn in the direction of this saving Christ, even in the wake of Jesus' miracle ministry!

Jesus wants us, even with our uncertainty. He hails John as an example for faithful following, despite his doubt. Praising his devotion, Jesus compliments John, saying there has never been anyone "greater than John the Baptist." Innocence, doubt, and bewilderment all seem to qualify as criteria for turning to Christ. Thanks be to God!

The Rev. Hillary T. West
Priest at Epiphany Episcopal Church
Herndon, Virginia

Questions

What are you expecting in the One who comes to save? What does Jesus expect of you?

Prayer

Lord, accept us in our doubts and wonders. May our innocence open us to the wisdom of your saving grace. Give us ears to listen. Soften our hearts to hold your redeeming love. Help us to expect the miracle of you in all that surrounds us. Amen.

Matthew 11:25—12:21

25At that time Jesus said, "I thank you, Father, Lord of heaven and earth, because you have hidden these things from the wise and the intelligent and have revealed them to infants; 26yes, Father, for such was your gracious will. 27All things have been handed over to me by my Father; and no one knows the Son except the Father, and no one knows the Father except the Son and anyone to whom the Son chooses to reveal him. 28"Come to me, all you that are weary and are carrying heavy burdens, and I will give you rest. 29Take my yoke upon you, and learn from me; for I am gentle and humble in heart, and you will find rest for your souls. 30For my yoke is easy, and my burden is light."

12 At that time Jesus went through the grainfields on the sabbath; his disciples were hungry, and they began to pluck heads of grain and to eat. 2When the Pharisees saw it, they said to him, "Look, your disciples are doing what is not lawful to do on the sabbath." 3He said to them, "Have you not read what David did when he and his companions were hungry? 4He entered the house of God and ate the bread of the Presence, which it was not lawful for him or his companions to eat, but only for the priests. 5Or have you not read in the law that on the sabbath the priests in the temple break the sabbath and yet are guiltless? 6I tell you, something greater than the temple is here. 7But if you had known what this means, 'I desire mercy and not sacrifice,' you would not have condemned the guiltless. 8For the Son of

Man is lord of the sabbath." ⁹He left that place and entered their synagogue; ¹⁰a man was there with a withered hand, and they asked him, "Is it lawful to cure on the sabbath?" so that they might accuse him. ¹¹He said to them, "Suppose one of you has only one sheep and it falls into a pit on the sabbath; will you not lay hold of it and lift it out? ¹²How much more valuable is a human being than a sheep! So it is lawful to do good on the sabbath." ¹³Then he said to the man, "Stretch out your hand." He stretched it out, and it was restored, as sound as the other.

¹⁴But the Pharisees went out and conspired against him, how to destroy him. ¹⁵When Jesus became aware of this, he departed. Many crowds followed him, and he cured all of them, ¹⁶and he ordered them not to make him known. ¹⁷This was to fulfill what had been spoken through the prophet Isaiah: ¹⁸"Here is my servant, whom I have chosen, my beloved, with whom my soul is well pleased. I will put my Spirit upon him, and he will proclaim justice to the Gentiles. ¹⁹He will not wrangle or cry aloud, nor will anyone hear his voice in the streets. ²⁰He will not break a bruised reed or quench a smoldering wick until he brings justice to victory. ²¹And in his name the Gentiles will hope."

Reflection

As our daughter was growing up, I had the good fortune of sewing most of her dresses. She'd watch, wondering how simple pieces of fabric could become a beautiful creation. Then, in the end, as I attached the skirt to the bodice and the sleeves to the shoulders, the entire dress came together with the yoke piece stretching from shoulder to shoulder. Once the yoke was in place, the dress was formed, given structure and identity.

Farm animals, when needing to pull or carry a cart or a plow, are yoked, harnessed together to better distribute the burden. Human yokes tend to be balanced across the shoulders to even the load. Jesus extends an invitation of relief as he says, "Take my yoke upon you, and learn from me."

Regardless of the relief we experience from yoking, we're still saddled with the imposition and inconvenience of our burdens. And these burdens, yoked or unyoked, can enslave us. Sharing Jesus' yoke implies that we are no longer enslaved by our burdens, but rather we're made free to serve our One True God in Jesus Christ.

Yokes instruct and discipline. Jesus' invitation is rooted in the ancient wisdom of the book of Sirach. In yoking ourselves with Christ, we embrace his wisdom and teaching, and in so doing, we find rest from our burdens. With Jesus, the yoke is easy, and our burden is light.

The Rev. Hillary T. West
Priest at Epiphany Episcopal Church
Herndon, Virginia

Question

What burdens might you yoke with Jesus in order to find rest?

Prayer

Lord of all, we give thanks for your invitation to relieve us from our burdens. Help us to trust in the power of your gentle goodness and grace. Deliver us from our weariness as we share our burdens with you and give us rest. Amen.

Matthew 12:22-45

²²Then they brought to him a demoniac who was blind and mute; and he cured him, so that the one who had been mute could speak and see. ²³All the crowds were amazed and said, "Can this be the Son of David?" ²⁴But when the Pharisees heard it, they said, "It is only by Beelzebul, the ruler of the demons, that this fellow casts out the demons." ²⁵He knew what they were thinking and said to them, "Every kingdom divided against itself is laid waste, and no city or house divided against itself will stand. ²⁶If Satan casts out Satan, he is divided against himself; how then will his kingdom stand? ²⁷If I cast out demons by Beelzebul, by whom do your own exorcists cast them out? Therefore they will be your judges. ²⁸But if it is by the Spirit of God that I cast out demons, then the kingdom of God has come to you. ²⁹Or how can one enter a strong man's house and plunder his property, without first tying up the strong man? Then indeed the house can be plundered. ³⁰Whoever is not with me is against me, and whoever does not gather with me scatters. ³¹Therefore I tell you, people will be forgiven for every sin and blasphemy, but blasphemy against the Spirit will not be forgiven. ³²Whoever speaks a word against the Son of Man will be forgiven, but whoever speaks against the Holy Spirit will not be forgiven, either in this age or in the age to come. ³³"Either make the tree good, and its fruit good; or make the tree bad, and its fruit bad; for the tree is known by its fruit. ³⁴You brood of vipers! How can you speak good things, when you are evil? For out of the abundance of the

heart the mouth speaks. ³⁵The good person brings good things out of a good treasure, and the evil person brings evil things out of an evil treasure. ³⁶I tell you, on the day of judgment you will have to give an account for every careless word you utter; ³⁷for by your words you will be justified, and by your words you will be condemned."

³⁸Then some of the scribes and Pharisees said to him, "Teacher, we wish to see a sign from you." ³⁹But he answered them, "An evil and adulterous generation asks for a sign, but no sign will be given to it except the sign of the prophet Jonah. ⁴⁰For just as Jonah was three days and three nights in the belly of the sea monster, so for three days and three nights the Son of Man will be in the heart of the earth. ⁴¹The people of Nineveh will rise up at the judgment with this generation and condemn it, because they repented at the proclamation of Jonah, and see, something greater than Jonah is here! ⁴²The queen of the South will rise up at the judgment with this generation and condemn it, because she came from the ends of the earth to listen to the wisdom of Solomon, and see, something greater than Solomon is here! ⁴³When the unclean spirit has gone out of a person, it wanders through waterless regions looking for a resting place, but it finds none. ⁴⁴Then it says, 'I will return to my house from which I came.' When it comes, it finds it empty, swept, and put in order. ⁴⁵Then it goes and brings along seven other spirits more evil than itself, and they enter and live there; and the last state of that person is worse than the first. So will it be also with this evil generation."

Reflection

Our passage starts with an act of compassion: Jesus heals a mentally disturbed man who is also blind and dumb. Not surprisingly, "all the crowds were amazed" and began to ask if Jesus might just be the one the Jews had been promised, the Messiah, or as they put it, "the Son of David."

If he were this one, then the power and influence of the religious leaders (the Pharisees and the scribes), who saw themselves as the guardians of the nation's development under God, would be challenged. So, they go on the offensive by turning an act of goodness into a demonic demonstration of power. They call white black and shut themselves off from seeing what is so obvious to the crowds—an act of divine goodness.

Jesus not only shows up the illogic of their assertions—"the tree is known by its fruit" but also castigates these religious leaders as "a brood of vipers" and "an evil and adulterous generation."

But it is easy to put passages like this into a box entitled "nasty things said about Jesus by evil religious leaders" and then move on. Is there a Pharisee or scribe gene in us? Are there times when we act as though we are so sure of our position that we miss seeing an act of goodness for what it is? Maybe we too fear our loss of power and influence.

Stephen Lyon
Author
London, England

Questions

What challenges does verse 36 present to you in your daily life? Does it call for any change in your behavior?

Prayer

O Lord, help me to see and thank you for evidence of your goodness in my life. Amen.

Matthew 12:46—13:23

⁴⁶While he was still speaking to the crowds, his mother and his brothers were standing outside, wanting to speak to him. ⁴⁷Someone told him, "Look, your mother and your brothers are standing outside, wanting to speak to you." ⁴⁸But to the one who had told him this, Jesus replied, "Who is my mother, and who are my brothers?" ⁴⁹And pointing to his disciples, he said, "Here are my mother and my brothers! ⁵⁰For whoever does the will of my Father in heaven is my brother and sister and mother."

13 That same day Jesus went out of the house and sat beside the sea. ²Such great crowds gathered around him that he got into a boat and sat there, while the whole crowd stood on the beach. ³And he told them many things in parables, saying: "Listen! A sower went out to sow. ⁴And as he sowed, some seeds fell on the path, and the birds came and ate them up. ⁵Other seeds fell on rocky ground, where they did not have much soil, and they sprang up quickly, since they had no depth of soil. ⁶But when the sun rose, they were scorched; and since they had no root, they withered away. ⁷Other seeds fell among thorns, and the thorns grew up and choked them. ⁸Other seeds fell on good soil and brought forth grain, some a hundredfold, some sixty, some thirty. ⁹Let anyone with ears listen!" ¹⁰Then the disciples came and asked him, "Why do you speak to them in parables?" ¹¹He answered, "To you it has been given to know the secrets of the kingdom of heaven, but to them it has not been given.

¹²"For to those who have, more will be given, and they will have an abundance; but from those who have nothing, even what they have will be taken away. ¹³The reason I speak to them in parables is that 'seeing they do not perceive, and hearing they do not listen, nor do they understand.' ¹⁴With them indeed is fulfilled the prophecy of Isaiah that says: 'You will indeed listen, but never understand, and you will indeed look, but never perceive. ¹⁵For this people's heart has grown dull, and their ears are hard of hearing, and they have shut their eyes; so that they might not look with their eyes, and listen with their ears, and understand with their heart and turn—and I would heal them.' ¹⁶But blessed are your eyes, for they see, and your ears, for they hear. ¹⁷Truly I tell you, many prophets and righteous people longed to see what you see, but did not see it, and to hear what you hear, but did not hear it.

¹⁸"Hear then the parable of the sower. ¹⁹When anyone hears the word of the kingdom and does not understand it, the evil one comes and snatches away what is sown in the heart; this is what was sown on the path. ²⁰As for what was sown on rocky ground, this is the one who hears the word and immediately receives it with joy; ²¹yet such a person has no root, but endures only for a while, and when trouble or persecution arises on account of the word, that person immediately falls away. ²²As for what was sown among thorns, this is the one who hears the word, but the cares of the world and the lure of wealth choke the word, and it yields nothing. ²³But as for what was sown on good soil, this is the one who hears the word and understands it, who indeed bears fruit and yields, in one case a hundredfold, in another sixty, and in another thirty."

Reflection

Today's passage relates one of the best known of Jesus' parables. It also gives us an insight into why he used this mode of teaching and the meaning of the parable of the sower. However, does its familiarity sometimes limit what we hear in the parable?

At first sight, we are offered four ways or modes of hearing the "word of the kingdom"—as a path, as rocky ground, as thorns, and as good soil. It does not require a degree in theology to see which way or mode Jesus wants us to adopt!

But there are two challenges we face. The first is where and when do we hear the word of the kingdom? When we read the Bible? Yes. When we hear a sermon? Yes. But that "word" might also come in everyday conversations, from seeing an act of goodness, from a picture or from creation. That leads us to the second challenge: Are we always ready to hear the word and understand it? Are we even always ready to recognize that we have heard the word of the kingdom?

My answer would have to be no at times. So maybe Jesus is describing four ways each one of us listens to the word, and the challenge is to recognize which mode we are in. Are we in path, rocky ground, thorn mode, or are we miles from the field? Are we ready to be like the good soil and hear?

Stephen Lyon
Author
London, England

Question _____

What are the things that get in the way of hearing the word of the kingdom that we need to recognize and address?

Prayer _____

O Lord, help us to clear the ground of our hearing so that your word can land on good soil. Amen.

Matthew 13:24-43

²⁴He put before them another parable: "The kingdom of heaven may be compared to someone who sowed good seed in his field; ²⁵but while everybody was asleep, an enemy came and sowed weeds among the wheat, and then went away. ²⁶So when the plants came up and bore grain, then the weeds appeared as well. ²⁷And the slaves of the householder came and said to him, 'Master, did you not sow good seed in your field? Where, then, did these weeds come from?' ²⁸He answered, 'An enemy has done this.' The slaves said to him, 'Then do you want us to go and gather them?' ²⁹But he replied, 'No; for in gathering the weeds you would uproot the wheat along with them. ³⁰Let both of them grow together until the harvest; and at harvest time I will tell the reapers, Collect the weeds first and bind them in bundles to be burned, but gather the wheat into my barn.'" ³¹He put before them another parable: "The kingdom of heaven is like a mustard seed that someone took and sowed in his field; ³²it is the smallest of all the seeds, but when it has grown it is the greatest of shrubs and becomes a tree, so that the birds of the air come and make nests in its branches." ³³He told them another parable: "The kingdom of heaven is like yeast that a woman took and mixed in with three measures of flour until all of it was leavened." ³⁴Jesus told the crowds all these things in parables; without a parable he told them nothing. ³⁵This was to fulfill what had been spoken through the prophet: "I will open my mouth to speak in parables; I will proclaim what has been

hidden from the foundation of the world." [36]Then he left the crowds and went into the house. And his disciples approached him, saying, "Explain to us the parable of the weeds of the field." [37]He answered, "The one who sows the good seed is the Son of Man; [38]the field is the world, and the good seed are the children of the kingdom; the weeds are the children of the evil one, [39]and the enemy who sowed them is the devil; the harvest is the end of the age, and the reapers are angels. [40]Just as the weeds are collected and burned up with fire, so will it be at the end of the age. [41]The Son of Man will send his angels, and they will collect out of his kingdom all causes of sin and all evildoers, [42]and they will throw them into the furnace of fire, where there will be weeping and gnashing of teeth. [43]Then the righteous will shine like the sun in the kingdom of their Father. Let anyone with ears listen!"

Reflection

Talking to a people oppressed in the midst of an occupied nation, our Lord speaks of seeds and weeds. It is powerful to consider the lilies of the field, the wonder of a mustard seed, and how weeds flourish. They teach us so much about how to cultivate the good in ourselves, the good around us, and to see the beauty and use of all creation.

There were no weeds in Eden, and even now, we are reminded not to judge the weeds against flowers. Weeds are part of the rhythm and truth of how everything on God's green earth is part of creation and can be used for the good. All we have to do is remember that even from small mustard seeds, beautiful shrubs can grow, changing the landscape.

The faith that Jesus is calling us to have is threefold: Faith that God will sort it out and all we have to do is love and tend the world; faith that the truth of how all things grow is true for even our small acts of love; and faith that we are part of a world created by a loving Creator who will not weed us out.

The Rev. Becca Stevens
Author and Founder of Magdalene House
Nashville, Tennessee

Questions _____

When you read this passage, do you see both weeds and wheat as part of the unfolding story of God's love for us?

What might that mean in your life?

Prayer _____

I am ready to keep climbing even though the mountain is steep. I am willing to keep searching even though the clouds are thick. I am able to keep praying even though the woods are flat. Take these offerings, my Lord, and use them so that I am surprised by what happens when I reach the top, and the clouds part. Amen.

Matthew 13:44-58

⁴⁴"The kingdom of heaven is like treasure hidden in a field, which someone found and hid; then in his joy he goes and sells all that he has and buys that field. ⁴⁵Again, the kingdom of heaven is like a merchant in search of fine pearls; ⁴⁶on finding one pearl of great value, he went and sold all that he had and bought it. ⁴⁷Again, the kingdom of heaven is like a net that was thrown into the sea and caught fish of every kind; ⁴⁸when it was full, they drew it ashore, sat down, and put the good into baskets but threw out the bad. ⁴⁹So it will be at the end of the age. The angels will come out and separate the evil from the righteous ⁵⁰and throw them into the furnace of fire, where there will be weeping and gnashing of teeth. ⁵¹Have you understood all this?" They answered, "Yes." ⁵²And he said to them, "Therefore every scribe who has been trained for the kingdom of heaven is like the master of a household who brings out of his treasure what is new and what is old."

⁵³When Jesus had finished these parables, he left that place. ⁵⁴He came to his hometown and began to teach the people in their synagogue, so that they were astounded and said, "Where did this man get this wisdom and these deeds of power? ⁵⁵Is not this the carpenter's son? Is not his mother called Mary? And are not his brothers James and Joseph and Simon and Judas? ⁵⁶And are not all his sisters with us? Where then did this man get all this?" ⁵⁷And they took offense at him. But Jesus said to them,

"Prophets are not without honor except in their own country and in their own house." [58]And he did not do many deeds of power there, because of their unbelief.

Reflection

The rapid pace of these parables gives us the impression that Jesus is going from town to town teaching and healing, and that he is in a hurry. Two thousand years later, we can feel that same urgency as we look around and see all the work there is to do. At the same time, we see the precious pearl of the gospel of love in the midst of it all. As disciples, we are called to do all we can to find the gospel and share it as our greatest treasure. Nowhere in the disciples' call does it say for us to try and make the world love us; instead, we are called to try and love the whole world for the sake of the gospel. It's a beautiful gift to find this treasure of the gospel in our lives; it is our calling to use our whole lives to live its message out in this world. That is how we can share the precious pearl.

The Rev. Becca Stevens
Author and Founder of Magdalene House
Nashville, Tennessee

Question _____

How do you see your community of faith collectively seeking the treasure and sharing it with the world?

Prayer _____

Gracious and loving Lord, we give you thanks for the weeds in our lives, the precious pearls, and the small mustard seeds. Awaken in us the truth to see your love in all things and in all people, and give us the will to live out your love in this world today. Amen.

Matthew 14:1-21

14At that time Herod the ruler heard reports about Jesus; ²and he said to his servants, "This is John the Baptist; he has been raised from the dead, and for this reason these powers are at work in him." ³For Herod had arrested John, bound him, and put him in prison on account of Herodias, his brother Philip's wife, ⁴because John had been telling him, "It is not lawful for you to have her." ⁵Though Herod wanted to put him to death, he feared the crowd, because they regarded him as a prophet. ⁶But when Herod's birthday came, the daughter of Herodias danced before the company, and she pleased Herod ⁷so much that he promised on oath to grant her whatever she might ask. ⁸Prompted by her mother, she said, "Give me the head of John the Baptist here on a platter." ⁹The king was grieved, yet out of regard for his oaths and for the guests, he commanded it to be given; ¹⁰he sent and had John beheaded in the prison. ¹¹The head was brought on a platter and given to the girl, who brought it to her mother. ¹²His disciples came and took the body and buried it; then they went and told Jesus.

¹³Now when Jesus heard this, he withdrew from there in a boat to a deserted place by himself. But when the crowds heard it, they followed him on foot from the towns. ¹⁴When he went ashore, he saw a great crowd; and he had compassion for them and cured their sick. ¹⁵When it was evening, the disciples came to him and said, "This is a deserted place, and the hour is now late; send the crowds away so that they may go into the villages

and buy food for themselves." ¹⁶Jesus said to them, "They need not go away; you give them something to eat." ¹⁷They replied, "We have nothing here but five loaves and two fish." ¹⁸And he said, "Bring them here to me." ¹⁹Then he ordered the crowds to sit down on the grass. Taking the five loaves and the two fish, he looked up to heaven, and blessed and broke the loaves, and gave them to the disciples, and the disciples gave them to the crowds. ²⁰And all ate and were filled; and they took up what was left over of the broken pieces, twelve baskets full. ²¹And those who ate were about five thousand men, besides women and children.

Reflection

I've never liked event planning, although I've done a fair amount, especially fundraisers. There are too many variables beyond my control: How many people will respond to the invitation? How much money will they donate? And, of course, how much food should I order? I'd just as soon take the disciples' approach and send them all home to fend for themselves.

Jesus, however, doesn't share my anxieties. Perhaps he already knows what I have learned over time: things will never go exactly as planned. More people will show up than expected or the food will be late or the keynote speaker will get stuck in traffic. No matter how hard you try, most things are beyond your control.

Herod, on the other hand, holds too hard to the fate of John the Baptist. He promises too much, believes too much in his own power. The harder we hold on to what we have and the more adamantly we deny the fact that this life can be unpredictable and surprising, the less room there is for the Spirit to move and the more likely the world will knock everything out of our grasp.

We do what we can to plan and to make the best use of what we've been given, but at a certain point we must remember that our influence in the world is small. We have to release our grip on our loaves and fishes in faith. They weren't really ours to begin with.

Jeremiah Sierra
Managing Editor at Trinity Wall Street
New York City, New York

Questions

What aspects of your life are you trying too hard to control? How might you loosen your grip?

Prayer

God, help us to remember that even the best-laid plans go awry and to release our false sense of control. Amen.

Matthew 14:22—15:11

^{22}Immediately he made the disciples get into the boat and go on ahead to the other side, while he dismissed the crowds. ^{23}And after he had dismissed the crowds, he went up the mountain by himself to pray. When evening came, he was there alone, ^{24}but by this time the boat, battered by the waves, was far from the land, for the wind was against them. ^{25}And early in the morning he came walking toward them on the sea. ^{26}But when the disciples saw him walking on the sea, they were terrified, saying, "It is a ghost!" And they cried out in fear. ^{27}But immediately Jesus spoke to them and said, "Take heart, it is I; do not be afraid." ^{28}Peter answered him, "Lord, if it is you, command me to come to you on the water." ^{29}He said, "Come." So Peter got out of the boat, started walking on the water, and came toward Jesus. ^{30}But when he noticed the strong wind, he became frightened, and beginning to sink, he cried out, "Lord, save me!" ^{31}Jesus immediately reached out his hand and caught him, saying to him, "You of little faith, why did you doubt?" ^{32}When they got into the boat, the wind ceased. ^{33}And those in the boat worshiped him, saying, "Truly you are the Son of God."

^{34}When they had crossed over, they came to land at Gennesaret. ^{35}After the people of that place recognized him, they sent word throughout the region and brought all who were sick to him, ^{36}and begged him that they might touch even the fringe of his cloak; and all who touched it were healed.

15 Then Pharisees and scribes came to Jesus from Jerusalem and said, [2]"Why do your disciples break the tradition of the elders? For they do not wash their hands before they eat." [3]He answered them, "And why do you break the commandment of God for the sake of your tradition? [4]For God said, 'Honor your father and your mother,' and, 'Whoever speaks evil of father or mother must surely die.' [5]But you say that whoever tells father or mother, 'Whatever support you might have had from me is given to God,' then that person need not honor the father. [6]So, for the sake of your tradition, you make void the word of God. [7]You hypocrites! Isaiah prophesied rightly about you when he said: [8]'This people honors me with their lips, but their hearts are far from me; [9]in vain do they worship me, teaching human precepts as doctrines.'"

[10]Then he called the crowd to him and said to them, "Listen and understand: [11]it is not what goes into the mouth that defiles a person, but it is what comes out of the mouth that defiles."

Reflection

There are questions that are asked in order to learn, and then there are questions asked to reveal what you already know. Other than perhaps Jesus and Plato, few people can ask the second type of question without sounding insufferable. Case in point is the Pharisees, who use their questions to entrap Jesus and demonstrate their supposed superiority. Of course, Jesus uses the opportunity to teach them anyway.

The scary thing about an honest question is that it opens us up to the truth, and the truth can be painful, especially when we are learning about the deepest parts of ourselves.

Asking a question without knowing the answer, learning about ourselves, and learning to love others is a bit like stepping out onto water. Fortunately, when we raise questions in the context of a loving relationship, we can trust that even when we are confronted by some difficult revelation about ourselves, we are loved anyway. We might discover cowardice or cruelty we didn't know we had in us or an inclination to miss the mark and hurt others, yet we know we are loved. This is something I have experienced again and again in my life. I will get it wrong. I will fail. I will still be loved.

We may begin to sink, but we can trust that some firm hand will grasp ours and pull us up, even while chastising us. Oh, you of little faith, it is good that you stepped out onto the waters.

Jeremiah Sierra
Managing Editor at Trinity Wall Street
New York City, New York

Question _____

What questions are you afraid to ask about your faith or other aspects of yourself?

Prayer _____

May we be open to asking difficult questions and learning difficult lessons, secure in the knowledge that we will always be loved. Amen.

Matthew 15:12-28

¹²Then the disciples approached and said to him, "Do you know that the Pharisees took offense when they heard what you said?" ¹³He answered, "Every plant that my heavenly Father has not planted will be uprooted. ¹⁴Let them alone; they are blind guides of the blind. And if one blind person guides another, both will fall into a pit." ¹⁵But Peter said to him, "Explain this parable to us." ¹⁶Then he said, "Are you also still without understanding? ¹⁷Do you not see that whatever goes into the mouth enters the stomach, and goes out into the sewer? ¹⁸But what comes out of the mouth proceeds from the heart, and this is what defiles. ¹⁹For out of the heart come evil intentions, murder, adultery, fornication, theft, false witness, slander.

²⁰These are what defile a person, but to eat with unwashed hands does not defile."

²¹Jesus left that place and went away to the district of Tyre and Sidon. ²²Just then a Canaanite woman from that region came out and started shouting, "Have mercy on me, Lord, Son of David; my daughter is tormented by a demon." ²³But he did not answer her at all. And his disciples came and urged him, saying, "Send her away, for she keeps shouting after us." ²⁴He answered, "I was sent only to the lost sheep of the house of Israel." ²⁵But she came and knelt before him, saying, "Lord, help me." ²⁶He answered, "It is not fair to take the children's food and throw it to the dogs." ²⁷She said, "Yes, Lord, yet even the dogs eat the crumbs that

fall from their masters' table." [28]Then Jesus answered her, "Woman, great is your faith! Let it be done for you as you wish." And her daughter was healed instantly.

Reflection

Verses 12-16 interrupt the flow of Jesus' teaching, and verse 11 connects to verse 17 so well. The interruption may be because something extraordinary has happened: the Pharisees have understood Jesus' parable, but the disciples haven't! This is contrary to the usual pattern in the gospels where even the mad can recognise Jesus as Messiah yet the "holy ones" cannot.

The Pharisees are not well-regarded by Jesus, but on this occasion, they have a clear understanding of what he has said and, equally clearly, see it as a threat to the very core of their thinking. Since what soils the body comes from outside, the Pharisees consider that the same is true for the soul. Jesus contradicts this by declaring that a person is defiled by words and actions that express thoughts.

In verses 21-28, we again meet a surprise. We, along with his disciples, expect Jesus to respond compassionately to the Canaanite mother, so we are shocked when Jesus doesn't answer her. The Jewish belief about defilement separated them from the Gentiles. Yet it is unexpected after his earlier remarks that Jesus raises this barrier to healing here—the barrier being that the family is not Jewish and therefore considered defiled. Yet the woman's faith surprises Jesus. He concedes to her request because out of her soul have come words and actions that identify her as undefiled by his own definition.

In these verses, we find things that are surprising and unexpected: the inherent quality of the Good News and the challenge to think differently about the God of surprises.

The Most Rev. Bolly anak Lapok
Archbishop of South East Asia
Kuching, Malaysia

Question

How much of our worry is attributable to our lack of faith in a God of surprises?

Prayer

Surprise us Lord, when we are too well-pleased with ourselves and when our dreams have come true because we have dreamed too little. Amen.

Matthew 15:29—16:12

²⁹After Jesus had left that place, he passed along the Sea of Galilee, and he went up the mountain, where he sat down. ³⁰Great crowds came to him, bringing with them the lame, the maimed, the blind, the mute, and many others. They put them at his feet, and he cured them, ³¹so that the crowd was amazed when they saw the mute speaking, the maimed whole, the lame walking, and the blind seeing. And they praised the God of Israel. ³²Then Jesus called his disciples to him and said, "I have compassion for the crowd, because they have been with me now for three days and have nothing to eat; and I do not want to send them away hungry, for they might faint on the way." ³³The disciples said to him, "Where are we to get enough bread in the desert to feed so great a crowd?" ³⁴Jesus asked them, "How many loaves have you?" They said, "Seven, and a few small fish." ³⁵Then ordering the crowd to sit down on the ground, ³⁶he took the seven loaves and the fish; and after giving thanks he broke them and gave them to the disciples, and the disciples gave them to the crowds. ³⁷And all of them ate and were filled; and they took up the broken pieces left over, seven baskets full. ³⁸Those who had eaten were four thousand men, besides women and children. ³⁹After sending away the crowds, he got into the boat and went to the region of Magadan.

16 The Pharisees and Sadducees came, and to test Jesus they asked him to show them a sign from heaven. ²He answered them, "When it is evening, you say, 'It will be

fair weather, for the sky is red.' ³And in the morning, 'It will be stormy today, for the sky is red and threatening.' You know how to interpret the appearance of the sky, but you cannot interpret the signs of the times. ⁴An evil and adulterous generation asks for a sign, but no sign will be given to it except the sign of Jonah." Then he left them and went away.

⁵When the disciples reached the other side, they had forgotten to bring any bread. ⁶Jesus said to them, "Watch out, and beware of the yeast of the Pharisees and Sadducees." ⁷They said to one another, "It is because we have brought no bread." ⁸And becoming aware of it, Jesus said, "You of little faith, why are you talking about having no bread? ⁹Do you still not perceive? Do you not remember the five loaves for the five thousand, and how many baskets you gathered? ¹⁰Or the seven loaves for the four thousand, and how many baskets you gathered?

¹¹How could you fail to perceive that I was not speaking about bread? Beware of the yeast of the Pharisees and Sadducees!" ¹²Then they understood that he had not told them to beware of the yeast of bread, but of the teaching of the Pharisees and Sadducees.

Reflection

The initial verses in this passage describe how Jesus healed, just as the Isaiah prophecy foretold of the Messiah's revealing work. In this way, Matthew sees this feeding as a sign pointing to the Messiah—an echo of what God did for the tribes who had escaped from Egypt.

Leaving to others the symbolism of the numbers in the story, a simple message comes that when people follow Jesus with enthusiasm (impulsively and so forgetting to take any food with them), he will provide them with what they need, and it will come from within their own ranks, whose meager but faithful offering will be made sufficient for all. This story inspires hope.

At a deeper level, Matthew sets the story against the background of a misunderstanding by the disciples after the event that turns on the word "yeast" (the element that makes bread rise). The disciples think Jesus is complaining about the bread they forgot to bring. Jesus puts them right, telling them that the teaching of the Sadducees and Pharisees that makes them prominent like risen bread is lethal, yet at the heart of Jesus' ministry is a teaching that really feeds souls.

Matthew questions his reader: Can you see the healing and so see the Messiah? Can you see the feeding and so see the Messiah? Or are you listening to teaching that seems reasonable but is actually dangerous and harmful?

The Most Rev. Bolly anak Lapok
Archbishop of South East Asia
Kuching, Malaysia

Questions

How can you guard against reasonable teaching and embrace a teaching that feeds your soul?

When have you followed Jesus with enthusiasm?

Prayer

God, give us grace to be open to your will, to recognize your faithful teaching, and to offer all we have to you, impulsively and with great generosity. Amen.

Matthew 16:13-28

¹³Now when Jesus came into the district of Caesarea Philippi, he asked his disciples, "Who do people say that the Son of Man is?" ¹⁴And they said, "Some say John the Baptist, but others Elijah, and still others Jeremiah or one of the prophets." ¹⁵He said to them, "But who do you say that I am?" ¹⁶Simon Peter answered, "You are the Messiah, the Son of the living God." ¹⁷And Jesus answered him, "Blessed are you, Simon son of Jonah! For flesh and blood has not revealed this to you, but my Father in heaven. ¹⁸And I tell you, you are Peter, and on this rock I will build my church, and the gates of Hades will not prevail against it. ¹⁹I will give you the keys of the kingdom of heaven, and whatever you bind on earth will be bound in heaven, and whatever you loose on earth will be loosed in heaven." ²⁰Then he sternly ordered the disciples not to tell anyone that he was the Messiah.

²¹From that time on, Jesus began to show his disciples that he must go to Jerusalem and undergo great suffering at the hands of the elders and chief priests and scribes, and be killed, and on the third day be raised. ²²And Peter took him aside and began to rebuke him, saying, "God forbid it, Lord! This must never happen to you." ²³But he turned and said to Peter, "Get behind me, Satan! You are a stumbling block to me; for you are setting your mind not on divine things but on human things."

²⁴Then Jesus told his disciples, "If any want to become my followers, let them deny themselves and take up their cross and follow me. ²⁵For those who want to save their life will

lose it, and those who lose their life for my sake will find it. ²⁶For what will it profit them if they gain the whole world but forfeit their life? Or what will they give in return for their life? ²⁷For the Son of Man is to come with his angels in the glory of his Father, and then he will repay everyone for what has been done. ²⁸Truly I tell you, there are some standing here who will not taste death before they see the Son of Man coming in his kingdom."

Reflection

Sometimes it is the question rather than the answer that advances our learning most. In much of Matthew's Gospel, disciples are characterized as those who listen and understand Jesus' teaching. The question-and-answer format in this passage between the disciples and Jesus, however, gives them a chance to speak their minds and hearts, not yet publicly, but within the intimate setting of teacher and disciples.

"Who do you say that I am?" is a question designed to help the disciples learn something more of Jesus. But importantly, at this critical juncture in the story, perhaps they need to learn something about themselves. Are they ready for what lies ahead? As they ponder all they have seen and heard, the disciples need to say what Jesus in his fullness is to them personally. This work of salvation has breadth in the ways it may be interpreted. At some point it must become a part of the heart, mind, and soul of the disciples. They cannot remain spectators to all they have seen and heard. They must understand themselves as part of the story.

The litmus test used by some Christians—"Do you accept Jesus as your Lord and Savior?"—can be judgmental and limiting, but the personal discernment and struggle in discovering one's answer is indeed a fruitful experience. The Holy Spirit moves in such a conversation with God, and we in turn discern the ways in which we are called to serve God's kingdom.

The Rt. Rev. Mary Gray-Reeves
Bishop of the Diocese of El Camino Real
Seaside, California

A Journey with Matthew

Questions

Who do you say Jesus is?

How does your understanding of Jesus and your relationship with him translate into service for the kingdom of God?

Prayer

O Jesus, revelation of grace, may our hearts, minds, and spirits be open to your fullness. May we embrace you as completely as you embrace us. Amen.

Matthew 17:1-20

17 Six days later, Jesus took with him Peter and James and his brother John and led them up a high mountain, by themselves. ²And he was transfigured before them, and his face shone like the sun, and his clothes became dazzling white. ³Suddenly there appeared to them Moses and Elijah, talking with him. ⁴Then Peter said to Jesus, "Lord, it is good for us to be here; if you wish, I will make three dwellings here, one for you, one for Moses, and one for Elijah." ⁵While he was still speaking, suddenly a bright cloud overshadowed them, and from the cloud a voice said, "This is my Son, the Beloved; with him I am well pleased; listen to him!" ⁶When the disciples heard this, they fell to the ground and were overcome by fear. ⁷But Jesus came and touched them, saying, "Get up and do not be afraid." ⁸And when they looked up, they saw no one except Jesus himself alone. ⁹As they were coming down the mountain, Jesus ordered them, "Tell no one about the vision until after the Son of Man has been raised from the dead." ¹⁰And the disciples asked him, "Why, then, do the scribes say that Elijah must come first?" ¹¹He replied, "Elijah is indeed coming and will restore all things; ¹²but I tell you that Elijah has already come, and they did not recognize him, but they did to him whatever they pleased. So also the Son of Man is about to suffer at their hands." ¹³Then the disciples understood that he was speaking to them about John the Baptist.

¹⁴When they came to the crowd, a man came to him, knelt before him, ¹⁵and said, "Lord, have

mercy on my son, for he is an epileptic and he suffers terribly; he often falls into the fire and often into the water. [16]And I brought him to your disciples, but they could not cure him." [17]Jesus answered, "You faithless and perverse generation, how much longer must I be with you? How much longer must I put up with you? Bring him here to me." [18]And Jesus rebuked the demon, and it came out of him, and the boy was cured instantly. [19]Then the disciples came to Jesus privately and said, "Why could we not cast it out?" [20]He said to them, "Because of your little faith. For truly I tell you, if you have faith the size of a mustard seed, you will say to this mountain, 'Move from here to there,' and it will move; and nothing will be impossible for you."

Reflection

The math of financial stewardship is easy when we earn little—and when what we do earn comes in a lump sum. When one has property, stocks, trusts, and other assets, calculating God's gifts to us requires more prayerful understanding so we can know what to give away. How and what do we calculate? The stewardship of spiritual experience is the same. Do we know and understand all the gifts God has revealed to us? Can we measure them?

Peter, James, and John witness the Transfiguration, a moment of glory not to be overlooked. It must be counted, understood. From the treasures of their Jewish heritage and the richness of their experience with Jesus, they seek to make sense of this vision. What is its purpose and its use? How does this vision fit into the story? Once again, Jesus calls them to confidentiality. This glorious moment must remain between teacher and disciples for now. It is not yet time to share what they have witnessed.

In the story of the child gripped by epilepsy that follows, lack of faith is the understanding Jesus offers for the disciples' inability to complete the healing. Jesus suggests it is not quantity but quality of faith that is required. Perhaps in order to make sense of visions of transfiguration, it is not a matter of intellectual understanding but of trusting the experience itself. Faith is trust; trust is faith.

The Rt. Rev. Mary Gray-Reeves
Bishop of the Diocese of El Camino Real
Seaside, California

A Journey with Matthew

Questions

What do the words understanding, faith, and trust mean to you?

Do you trust your experience with Jesus even if you do not always understand it?

Prayer

O God, source of all wisdom, may we trust you even when we cannot explain you. Amen.

Matthew 17:22—18:14

²²As they were gathering in Galilee, Jesus said to them, "The Son of Man is going to be betrayed into human hands, ²³and they will kill him, and on the third day he will be raised." And they were greatly distressed.

²⁴When they reached Capernaum, the collectors of the temple tax came to Peter and said, "Does your teacher not pay the temple tax?" ²⁵He said, "Yes, he does." And when he came home, Jesus spoke of it first, asking, "What do you think, Simon? From whom do kings of the earth take toll or tribute? From their children or from others?" ²⁶When Peter said, "From others," Jesus said to him, "Then the children are free. ²⁷However, so that we do not give offense to them, go to the sea and cast a hook; take the first fish that comes up; and when you open its mouth, you will find a coin; take that and give it to them for you and me."

18 At that time the disciples came to Jesus and asked, "Who is the greatest in the kingdom of heaven?" ²He called a child, whom he put among them, ³and said, "Truly I tell you, unless you change and become like children, you will never enter the kingdom of heaven. ⁴Whoever becomes humble like this child is the greatest in the kingdom of heaven. ⁵Whoever welcomes one such child in my name welcomes me. ⁶"If any of you put a stumbling block before one of these little ones who believe in me, it would be better for you if a great millstone were fastened around your neck and you were drowned in the depth of the sea.

[7]"Woe to the world because of stumbling blocks! Occasions for stumbling are bound to come, but woe to the one by whom the stumbling block comes! [8]If your hand or your foot causes you to stumble, cut it off and throw it away; it is better for you to enter life maimed or lame than to have two hands or two feet and to be thrown into the eternal fire. [9]And if your eye causes you to stumble, tear it out and throw it away; it is better for you to enter life with one eye than to have two eyes and to be thrown into the hell of fire. [10]Take care that you do not despise one of these little ones; for, I tell you, in heaven their angels continually see the face of my Father in heaven. [12]What do you think? If a shepherd has a hundred sheep, and one of them has gone astray, does he not leave the ninety-nine on the mountains and go in search of the one that went astray? [13]And if he finds it, truly I tell you, he rejoices over it more than over the ninety-nine that never went astray. [14]So it is not the will of your Father in heaven that one of these little ones should be lost."

Reflection

Jesus tells us that we need to become like children. Some years ago, when our youngest daughter was three or four years old, I was getting ready to take her to preschool. It was a moderately clear day, not particularly overcast. The weather report forecast thunderstorms and rain. When I asked our daughter to put on her raincoat, she suggested that she wear something else because it wasn't raining. I said it was going to rain later in the day. She asked me how I knew that, and I explained to her how I had watched Al Roker on the weather report, and he said it was going to rain. I tried to explain it to her, but somehow she had it in her head that it wasn't going to rain because it wasn't raining at that moment. Eventually I just made her wear her raincoat.

Later I had to laugh because on some level I suspect that's how we must look to God when we want to live life our way instead of God's way. Acknowledging this is not a matter of childish immaturity, but mature and healthy self-awareness. Acknowledging this and then being open to learn from the God who created us is indeed the beginning of wisdom, and where wisdom is, the kingdom of God is just off that horizon.

The Rt. Rev. Michael Curry
Bishop of the Diocese of North Carolina
Charlotte, North Carolina

A Journey with Matthew

Question

What is one thing you can do today to open yourself to God's guidance and direction?

Prayer

Almighty God, help us to see beyond our childish ways so that we may seek and serve you with gladness of heart. Amen.

Matthew 18:15-35

¹⁵"If another member of the church sins against you, go and point out the fault when the two of you are alone. If the member listens to you, you have regained that one. ¹⁶But if you are not listened to, take one or two others along with you, so that every word may be confirmed by the evidence of two or three witnesses. ¹⁷If the member refuses to listen to them, tell it to the church; and if the offender refuses to listen even to the church, let such a one be to you as a Gentile and a tax collector. ¹⁸Truly I tell you, whatever you bind on earth will be bound in heaven, and whatever you loose on earth will be loosed in heaven. ¹⁹Again, truly I tell you, if two of you agree on earth about anything you ask, it will be done for you by my Father in heaven. ²⁰For where two or three are gathered in my name, I am there among them."

²¹Then Peter came and said to him, "Lord, if another member of the church sins against me, how often should I forgive? As many as seven times?" ²²Jesus said to him, "Not seven times, but, I tell you, seventy-seven times. ²³"For this reason the kingdom of heaven may be compared to a king who wished to settle accounts with his slaves. ²⁴When he began the reckoning, one who owed him ten thousand talents was brought to him; ²⁵and, as he could not pay, his lord ordered him to be sold, together with his wife and children and all his possessions, and payment to be made. ²⁶So the slave fell on his knees before him, saying, 'Have patience with me, and I will

pay you everything.' 27And out of pity for him, the lord of that slave released him and forgave him the debt. 28But that same slave, as he went out, came upon one of his fellow slaves who owed him a hundred denarii; and seizing him by the throat, he said, 'Pay what you owe.' 29Then his fellow slave fell down and pleaded with him, 'Have patience with me, and I will pay you.' 30But he refused; then he went and threw him into prison until he would pay the debt. 31When his fellow slaves saw what had happened, they were greatly distressed, and they went and reported to their lord all that had taken place. 32Then his lord summoned him and said to him, 'You wicked slave! I forgave you all that debt because you pleaded with me. 33Should you not have had mercy on your fellow slave, as I had mercy on you?' 34And in anger his lord handed him over to be tortured until he would pay his entire debt. 35So my heavenly Father will also do to every one of you, if you do not forgive your brother or sister from your heart."

Reflection

The late Dr. Benjamin Elijah Mays, sometime president of Morehouse College in Atlanta, was fond of saying "faith is taking your best step and leaving the rest to God." Faith is giving it your best, and letting God do the rest.

Sometimes that trust takes the shape of risking rejection in order to repair or reconcile a broken relationship. That, in part, seems to be what Jesus is getting at when he teaches his followers to seek reconciliation whenever there is brokenness or estrangement in the community of faith. That can be risky business. But reconciliation is worth the risk.

Only when every reasonable effort has failed, do you just let it be. Here is where Jesus offers a powerful insight: When all efforts at reconciliation fail, let go. "Let go and let God," as the saying goes. Where that may go is no longer in our hands. And then, who knows what the future will bring? That's faith. "Faith is taking your best step and leaving the rest to God."

The Rt. Rev. Michael Curry
Bishop of the Diocese of North Carolina
Charlotte, North Carolina

Question

Can you think of a time or occasion when seeking reconciliation called forth such faith from you?

Prayer

Have thine own way, Lord, have thine own way.
Thou art the potter, I am the clay.
Mold me and make me, after thy will.
While I am waiting, yielded and still. Amen.

Matthew 19:1-22

19 When Jesus had finished saying these things, he left Galilee and went to the region of Judea beyond the Jordan. ²Large crowds followed him, and he cured them there.

³Some Pharisees came to him, and to test him they asked, "Is it lawful for a man to divorce his wife for any cause?" ⁴He answered, "Have you not read that the one who made them at the beginning 'made them male and female,' ⁵and said, 'For this reason a man shall leave his father and mother and be joined to his wife, and the two shall become one flesh'? ⁶So they are no longer two, but one flesh. Therefore what God has joined together, let no one separate." ⁷They said to him, "Why then did Moses command us to give a certificate of dismissal and to divorce her?" ⁸He said to them,

"It was because you were so hard-hearted that Moses allowed you to divorce your wives, but from the beginning it was not so. ⁹And I say to you, whoever divorces his wife, except for unchastity, and marries another commits adultery." ¹⁰His disciples said to him, "If such is the case of a man with his wife, it is better not to marry." ¹¹But he said to them, "Not everyone can accept this teaching, but only those to whom it is given. ¹²For there are eunuchs who have been so from birth, and there are eunuchs who have been made eunuchs by others, and there are eunuchs who have made themselves eunuchs for the sake of the kingdom of heaven. Let anyone accept this who can."

¹³Then little children were being brought to him in order that he might lay his hands on them

and pray. The disciples spoke sternly to those who brought them; [14]but Jesus said, "Let the little children come to me, and do not stop them; for it is to such as these that the kingdom of heaven belongs." [15]And he laid his hands on them and went on his way.

[16]Then someone came to him and said, "Teacher, what good deed must I do to have eternal life?" [17]And he said to him, "Why do you ask me about what is good? There is only one who is good. If you wish to enter into life, keep the commandments." [18]He said to him, "Which ones?" And Jesus said, "You shall not murder; You shall not commit adultery; You shall not steal; You shall not bear false witness; [19]Honor your father and mother; also, You shall love your neighbor as yourself." [20]The young man said to him, "I have kept all these; what do I still lack?" [21]Jesus said to him, "If you wish to be perfect, go, sell your possessions, and give the money to the poor, and you will have treasure in heaven; then come, follow me." [22]When the young man heard this word, he went away grieving, for he had many possessions.

Reflection

Relationships matter deeply; family relationships have a particularly high priority. Yet they are not the ultimate relationships with which we are all concerned.

In some parts of Jewish society, it had become easy for a man to end a marriage. Here Jesus makes it clear he is on the side of wives and of lifelong, faithful marriage. By making it clear that easy divorce for men was unacceptable, Jesus was protecting the lives and reputations of the women who had no say. He reaffirms that from the beginning of humanity, God's intention is the joining of man and woman as one flesh. But Jesus then makes it clear that marriage is not for everyone; there are "eunuchs who have made themselves a eunuch for the sake of the kingdom of heaven."

Then in blessing small children, against the disciples' thinking, Jesus makes it clear just how important they are so far as God's kingdom is concerned. Yet having blessed them, he leaves them with their parents; this parent-child relationship matters.

It mattered to the rich young ruler. He had been a good son—indeed he had been a good person. But along the way, his riches squeezed out God. Jesus challenged him to get his relationships right, to realize that God matters more than anything or anyone.

All of our relationships, in marriage, as single people, as children, and with material things must be lived in the light of our relationship with God and the kingdom.

The Rt. Rev. Paul Butler
Bishop of Durham
Nottinghamshire, England

A Journey with Matthew

Questions

What relationships matter most to you?

How do they reflect the life of God's kingdom?

Prayer

Relating God, help us to relate well to all people so that the blessing of your kingdom may come. Amen.

Matthew 19:23—20:16

²³Then Jesus said to his disciples, "Truly I tell you, it will be hard for a rich person to enter the kingdom of heaven. ²⁴Again I tell you, it is easier for a camel to go through the eye of a needle than for someone who is rich to enter the kingdom of God." ²⁵When the disciples heard this, they were greatly astounded and said, "Then who can be saved?" ²⁶But Jesus looked at them and said, "For mortals it is impossible, but for God all things are possible." ²⁷Then Peter said in reply, "Look, we have left everything and followed you. What then will we have?" ²⁸Jesus said to them, "Truly I tell you, at the renewal of all things, when the Son of Man is seated on the throne of his glory, you who have followed me will also sit on twelve thrones, judging the twelve tribes of Israel. ²⁹And everyone who has left houses or brothers or sisters or father or mother or children or fields, for my name's sake, will receive a hundredfold, and will inherit eternal life. ³⁰But many who are first will be last, and the last will be first.

20 "For the kingdom of heaven is like a landowner who went out early in the morning to hire laborers for his vineyard. ²After agreeing with the laborers for the usual daily wage, he sent them into his vineyard. ³When he went out about nine o'clock, he saw others standing idle in the marketplace; ⁴and he said to them, 'You also go into the vineyard, and I will pay you whatever is right.' So they went. ⁵When he went out again about noon and about three o'clock, he did the same. ⁶And about five o'clock he went

out and found others standing around; and he said to them, 'Why are you standing here idle all day?' ⁷They said to him, 'Because no one has hired us.' He said to them, 'You also go into the vineyard.' ⁸When evening came, the owner of the vineyard said to his manager, 'Call the laborers and give them their pay, beginning with the last and then going to the first.' ⁹When those hired about five o'clock came, each of them received the usual daily wage. ¹⁰Now when the first came, they thought they would receive more; but each of them also received the usual daily wage. ¹¹And when they received it, they grumbled against the landowner, ¹²saying, 'These last worked only one hour, and you have made them equal to us who have borne the burden of the day and the scorching heat.' ¹³But he replied to one of them, 'Friend, I am doing you no wrong; did you not agree with me for the usual daily wage? ¹⁴Take what belongs to you and go; I choose to give to this last the same as I give to you. ¹⁵Am I not allowed to do what I choose with what belongs to me? Or are you envious because I am generous?' ¹⁶So the last will be first, and the first will be last."

Reflection

Generosity is God's hallmark. Full of loving kindness, God generously gives and gives again.

We all become caught up in working for the kingdom. We start thinking that we deserve some extra reward for our sacrifice, our hard work. We become jealous of those who seem to have it all from God without having put in the hard yards. We so readily forget that it is all of grace: Every one of the labourers was only there because of the owner's generosity; none had done it alone.

Following Jesus is costly. It involves sacrifice, hardship, loss, pain, and difficulty. It is the Way of the Cross. This is the reality for many Christians through history and in many parts of our world today. When I think of some of the demands made on me, they pale in comparison to the plight of brothers and sisters who face real persecution and deprivation. I catch myself occasionally thinking that perhaps it is time for a little reward for all my hard work and effort. But none of us can tell God what our particular labours and sacrifices deserve by way of reward. At the final count, it is all entirely of God's grace and generosity alone. God decides the first and the last, and does so not by our justice but by amazing, wonderful grace.

The Rt. Rev. Paul Butler
Bishop of Durham
Nottinghamshire, England

A Journey with Matthew

Questions

Why do we persist in thinking that the kingdom is easier for the rich?

What labour is God calling you to today?

Prayer

Generous God, we are amazed by your great grace. Hallelujah! Help us to live in and by grace every day. Amen.

Matthew 20:17-34

17While Jesus was going up to Jerusalem, he took the twelve disciples aside by themselves, and said to them on the way, 18"See, we are going up to Jerusalem, and the Son of Man will be handed over to the chief priests and scribes, and they will condemn him to death; 19then they will hand him over to the Gentiles to be mocked and flogged and crucified; and on the third day he will be raised."

20Then the mother of the sons of Zebedee came to him with her sons, and kneeling before him, she asked a favor of him. 21And he said to her, "What do you want?" She said to him, "Declare that these two sons of mine will sit, one at your right hand and one at your left, in your kingdom." 22But Jesus answered, "You do not know what you are asking. Are you able to drink the cup that I am about to drink?" They said to him, "We are able." 23He said to them, "You will indeed drink my cup, but to sit at my right hand and at my left, this is not mine to grant, but it is for those for whom it has been prepared by my Father." 24When the ten heard it, they were angry with the two brothers. 25But Jesus called them to him and said, "You know that the rulers of the Gentiles lord it over them, and their great ones are tyrants over them. 26It will not be so among you; but whoever wishes to be great among you must be your servant, 27and whoever wishes to be first among you must be your slave; 28just as the Son of Man came not to be served but to serve, and to give his life a ransom for many."

[29]As they were leaving Jericho, a large crowd followed him. [30]There were two blind men sitting by the roadside. When they heard that Jesus was passing by, they shouted, "Lord, have mercy on us, Son of David!" [31]The crowd sternly ordered them to be quiet; but they shouted even more loudly, "Have mercy on us, Lord, Son of David!" [32]Jesus stood still and called them, saying, "What do you want me to do for you?" [33]They said to him, "Lord, let our eyes be opened." [34]Moved with compassion, Jesus touched their eyes. Immediately they regained their sight and followed him.

Reflection

We all know what it is like to share news with people, particularly news others may not be eager to hear. In this passage, the news is fully revealed by Jesus regarding his fate: He will be delivered over to the chief priests and teachers, who will condemn him to death; he will suffer death at the hands of Gentile rulers; and he will be raised to life on the third day.

But the news does not stop there. The mother of the sons of Zebedee asks Jesus to ensure that her sons will possess a privileged place in Jesus' kingdom. Here, again, in Jesus' reply, we hear news that may not be what she, or her sons, are expecting. It is not my call, Jesus tells her, to determine who sits where in this kingdom.

Such news stands in stark contrast to the expectations of the day, that the Messiah's coming would be one of triumph. Disappointing news indeed, certainly the opposite of what so many were anticipating.

Those who assume that the gospel of Jesus is shrouded in fantasy are in for a surprise: this gospel is grounded in reality, harsh reality in fact. Jesus' mission is far from otherworldly; in fact it brings us back, through suffering, to the concrete and the everyday.

Yet there is good news in that reality. A concrete gospel message is one that can be responsive to real needs of human beings, including the need of the two blind men to receive their sight.

The Rev. Daniel R. Heischman
Executive Director of the
National Association of Episcopal Schools
New York City, New York

Questions

What might be your experience of the gospel as "bad news?"

How does Jesus' message bring us back to reality, in our individual and collective lives?

Prayer

God, help us to bear the bad news with the good for the sake of your kingdom. Amen.

Matthew 21:1-22

21 When they had come near Jerusalem and had reached Bethphage, at the Mount of Olives, Jesus sent two disciples, [2]saying to them, "Go into the village ahead of you, and immediately you will find a donkey tied, and a colt with her; untie them and bring them to me. [3]If anyone says anything to you, just say this, 'The Lord needs them.' And he will send them immediately." [4]This took place to fulfill what had been spoken through the prophet, saying, [5]"Tell the daughter of Zion, Look, your king is coming to you, humble, and mounted on a donkey, and on a colt, the foal of a donkey." [6]The disciples went and did as Jesus had directed them; [7]they brought the donkey and the colt, and put their cloaks on them, and he sat on them. [8]A very large crowd spread their cloaks on the road, and others cut branches from the trees and spread them on the road. [9]The crowds that went ahead of him and that followed were shouting, "Hosanna to the Son of David! Blessed is the one who comes in the name of the Lord! Hosanna in the highest heaven!" [10]When he entered Jerusalem, the whole city was in turmoil, asking, "Who is this?" [11]The crowds were saying, "This is the prophet Jesus from Nazareth in Galilee."

[12]Then Jesus entered the temple and drove out all who were selling and buying in the temple, and he overturned the tables of the money changers and the seats of those who sold doves. [13]He said to them, "It is written, 'My house shall be called a house of prayer'; but you are making it a den of robbers."

¹⁴The blind and the lame came to him in the temple, and he cured them. ¹⁵But when the chief priests and the scribes saw the amazing things that he did, and heard the children crying out in the temple, "Hosanna to the Son of David," they became angry ¹⁶and said to him, "Do you hear what these are saying?" Jesus said to them, "Yes; have you never read, 'Out of the mouths of infants and nursing babies you have prepared praise for yourself'?" ¹⁷He left them, went out of the city to Bethany, and spent the night there.

¹⁸In the morning, when he returned to the city, he was hungry. ¹⁹And seeing a fig tree by the side of the road, he went to it and found nothing at all on it but leaves. Then he said to it, "May no fruit ever come from you again!" And the fig tree withered at once. ²⁰When the disciples saw it, they were amazed, saying, "How did the fig tree wither at once?" ²¹Jesus answered them, "Truly I tell you, if you have faith and do not doubt, not only will you do what has been done to the fig tree, but even if you say to this mountain, 'Be lifted up and thrown into the sea,' it will be done. ²²Whatever you ask for in prayer with faith, you will receive."

Reflection

As I read through Matthew's account of the early parts of the passion narrative, I am struck by the degree to which all of these events are so rooted in Hebrew tradition. Much of what is done is portrayed as fulfillment of scripture. While new things are happening—the Messiah is to suffer, compared with being triumphant—the story of Christ's passion is deeply embedded in the tradition from which Jesus and his disciples come.

Someone wise once told me that we become more and more like our parents the older we get. As much as we prefer to see ourselves as blazing our own trails, being individuals on our own, we are never really able to shed the customs and characteristics that are part of our background.

Today there is much talk and emphasis upon what the Christian religion is not. We take great pains to portray ourselves as being different from the common, traditional perceptions of what "religious people" do and believe. However, Matthew reminds us that as much as Jesus was doing a new thing, he—and we—never really venture that far from our roots. Indeed, those roots give shape, meaning, and distinctive identity to our present selves.

Our roots always call us back; they can also assist us in going forward.

The Rev. Daniel R. Heischman
Executive Director of the
National Association of Episcopal Schools
New York City, New York

Questions

Why might Hebrew tradition be important to Matthew as he recounts Jesus' passion?

What are the strands of our roots, our past, that surprise us by never really going away?

Prayer

God, help us to give thanks for our roots, and be aware of how they have shaped us into the people we are today. Amen.

Matthew 21:23-46

23When he entered the temple, the chief priests and the elders of the people came to him as he was teaching, and said, "By what authority are you doing these things, and who gave you this authority?" 24Jesus said to them, "I will also ask you one question; if you tell me the answer, then I will also tell you by what authority I do these things. 25Did the baptism of John come from heaven, or was it of human origin?" And they argued with one another, "If we say, 'From heaven,' he will say to us, 'Why then did you not believe him?' 26But if we say, 'Of human origin,' we are afraid of the crowd; for all regard John as a prophet." 27So they answered Jesus, "We do not know." And he said to them, "Neither will I tell you by what authority I am doing these things.

28"What do you think? A man had two sons; he went to the first and said, 'Son, go and work in the vineyard today.' 29He answered, 'I will not'; but later he changed his mind and went. 30The father went to the second and said the same; and he answered, 'I go, sir'; but he did not go. 31Which of the two did the will of his father?" They said, "The first." Jesus said to them, "Truly I tell you, the tax collectors and the prostitutes are going into the kingdom of God ahead of you. 32For John came to you in the way of righteousness and you did not believe him, but the tax collectors and the prostitutes believed him; and even after you saw it, you did not change your minds and believe him.

³³"Listen to another parable. There was a landowner who planted a vineyard, put a fence around it, dug a wine press in it, and built a watchtower. Then he leased it to tenants and went to another country. ³⁴When the harvest time had come, he sent his slaves to the tenants to collect his produce. ³⁵But the tenants seized his slaves and beat one, killed another, and stoned another. ³⁶Again he sent other slaves, more than the first; and they treated them in the same way. ³⁷Finally he sent his son to them, saying, 'They will respect my son.' ³⁸But when the tenants saw the son, they said to themselves, 'This is the heir; come, let us kill him and get his inheritance." ³⁹So they seized him, threw him out of the vineyard, and killed him. ⁴⁰Now when the owner of the vineyard comes, what will he do to those tenants?" ⁴¹They said to him, "He will put those wretches to a miserable death, and lease the vineyard to other tenants who will give him the produce at the harvest time." ⁴²Jesus said to them, "Have you never read in the scriptures: 'The stone that the builders rejected has become the cornerstone; this was the Lord's doing, and it is amazing in our eyes'? ⁴³Therefore I tell you, the kingdom of God will be taken away from you and given to a people that produces the fruits of the kingdom. ⁴⁴The one who falls on this stone will be broken to pieces; and it will crush anyone on whom it falls." ⁴⁵When the chief priests and the Pharisees heard his parables, they realized that he was speaking about them. ⁴⁶They wanted to arrest him, but they feared the crowds, because they regarded him as a prophet.

Reflection

The parable of the wicked tenants is found in very similar form in Mark and Luke. The parables of Jesus are lifelike stories. But Matthew's version of this story has features that do not seem very believable at all. Why would the tenants of this vineyard think that by murdering the owner's son, they could become the owners themselves? The property law that would allow such a thing has not yet been invented. And why would the owner risk sending his son into such a dangerous situation when his servants have been killed already? We don't notice how implausible these things are because we make the connection so quickly with God sending his son Jesus Christ into a dangerous and cruel world. The chief priests and the Pharisees, we are told, knew this parable was aimed at them. But can we be comfortable as followers of Jesus Christ that we have not treated him cruelly or, perhaps worse, allowed him to die in us through neglect?

The parable of the two sons is, by contrast, very lifelike and only to be found in Matthew's Gospel. In another vineyard, the owner asks his two sons to work for him for a day. One says he will and doesn't do it. The other says he won't and then changes his mind. How often do we promise and not deliver? How often does guilt get the better of us so that we eventually do the right thing? Humanity is fickle. But God is faithful and never gives up on the vineyard. For it to flourish, though, our response to God's love is needed.

The Rt. Rev. Graham James
Bishop of Norwich
Norwich, England

A Journey with Matthew

Questions

Which of the two sons in the parable is most like you?

What may you do to be more consistent in your response to God?

Prayer

Faithful God, forgive our fickleness and strengthen our will to respond in obedient love to your son Jesus Christ. Amen.

Matthew 22:1-22

22 Once more Jesus spoke to them in parables, saying: ²"The kingdom of heaven may be compared to a king who gave a wedding banquet for his son. ³He sent his slaves to call those who had been invited to the wedding banquet, but they would not come. ⁴Again he sent other slaves, saying, 'Tell those who have been invited: Look, I have prepared my dinner, my oxen and my fat calves have been slaughtered, and everything is ready; come to the wedding banquet.' ⁵But they made light of it and went away, one to his farm, another to his business, ⁶while the rest seized his slaves, mistreated them, and killed them. ⁷The king was enraged. He sent his troops, destroyed those murderers, and burned their city. ⁸Then he said to his slaves, 'The wedding is ready, but those invited were not worthy. ⁹Go therefore into the main streets, and invite everyone you find to the wedding banquet.' ¹⁰Those slaves went out into the streets and gathered all whom they found, both good and bad; so the wedding hall was filled with guests. ¹¹But when the king came in to see the guests, he noticed a man there who was not wearing a wedding robe, ¹²and he said to him, 'Friend, how did you get in here without a wedding robe?' And he was speechless. ¹³Then the king said to the attendants, 'Bind him hand and foot, and throw him into the outer darkness, where there will be weeping and gnashing of teeth.' ¹⁴For many are called, but few are chosen."

¹⁵Then the Pharisees went and plotted to entrap him in what he said. ¹⁶So they sent

their disciples to him, along with the Herodians, saying, "Teacher, we know that you are sincere, and teach the way of God in accordance with truth, and show deference to no one; for you do not regard people with partiality. [17]Tell us, then, what you think. Is it lawful to pay taxes to the emperor, or not?" [18]But Jesus, aware of their malice, said, "Why are you putting me to the test, you hypocrites? [19]Show me the coin used for the tax." And they brought him a denarius. [20]Then he said to them, "Whose head is this, and whose title?" [21]They answered, "The emperor's." Then he said to them, "Give therefore to the emperor the things that are the emperor's, and to God the things that are God's." [22]When they heard this, they were amazed; and they left him and went away.

Reflection

Matthew seems to be in the habit of making the lifelike parables of Jesus just a bit less believable. In Luke's version of the parable of the wedding feast, the guests all offer plausible excuses. One has bought a field and needs to look over it. Another has purchased some oxen. The third cannot leave his new wife. In Matthew's version, the guests don't even offer polite excuses. Some even kill the servants sent out with the invitations. So the angry king gives the order that all and sundry should share the wedding feast.

Then worse follows. The king notices a man who isn't wearing suitable clothes for a wedding. He expels him violently. But how could the poor man have been well-dressed, since he was brought in unexpectedly from the fields?

We mistake the meaning of the parable if we think it has much to do with wedding etiquette. Rather, the passage is about our preparation for God's coming kingdom. The followers of Jesus should be prepared at all times for the heavenly banquet. But how? By clothing ourselves with repentance and humility. Then we will never be surprised. Within the Christian family, we are even given the spiritual clothes to wear. We are called to pray on our knees. We are invited to worship with ears open to God's word. We extend our hands to receive the Body of Christ in Holy Communion. Our lips partake of the wine of his new life. The Christian life consists in constant and repeated preparation to meet God. The spiritual garments are available. It's putting them on day by day that's the challenge.

The Rt. Rev. Graham James
Bishop of Norwich
Norwich, England

Questions

What's the state of your wedding garment?

What can you do to keep your spiritual clothes in good order?

Prayer

Eternal God, in Jesus you invite us to your Kingdom. Clothe us with your grace that we may respond with joy. Amen.

Matthew 22:23-46

²³The same day some Sadducees came to him, saying there is no resurrection; and they asked him a question, saying, ²⁴"Teacher, Moses said, 'If a man dies childless, his brother shall marry the widow, and raise up children for his brother.' ²⁵Now there were seven brothers among us; the first married, and died childless, leaving the widow to his brother. ²⁶The second did the same, so also the third, down to the seventh. ²⁷Last of all, the woman herself died. ²⁸In the resurrection, then, whose wife of the seven will she be? For all of them had married her." ²⁹Jesus answered them, "You are wrong, because you know neither the scriptures nor the power of God. ³⁰For in the resurrection they neither marry nor are given in marriage, but are like angels in heaven. ³¹And as for the resurrection of the dead, have you not read what was said to you by God, ³²'I am the God of Abraham, the God of Isaac, and the God of Jacob'? He is God not of the dead, but of the living." ³³And when the crowd heard it, they were astounded at his teaching.

³⁴When the Pharisees heard that he had silenced the Sadducees, they gathered together, ³⁵and one of them, a lawyer, asked him a question to test him. ³⁶"Teacher, which commandment in the law is the greatest?" ³⁷He said to him, "'You shall love the Lord your God with all your heart, and with all your soul, and with all your mind.' ³⁸This is the greatest and first commandment. ³⁹And a second is like it: 'You shall love your neighbor as yourself.' ⁴⁰On these two commandments hang all the law and the prophets."

⁴¹Now while the Pharisees were gathered together, Jesus asked them this question: ⁴²"What do you think of the Messiah? Whose son is he?" They said to him, "The son of David." ⁴³He said to them, "How is it then that David by the Spirit calls him Lord, saying, ⁴⁴'The Lord said to my Lord, "Sit at my right hand, until I put your enemies under your feet"'? ⁴⁵If David thus calls him Lord, how can he be his son?" ⁴⁶No one was able to give him an answer, nor from that day did anyone dare to ask him any more questions.

Reflection

The Sadducees with their set minds come to Jesus with a test question to make the resurrection look ridiculous. Unlike the Pharisees—who believe in the resurrection of the dead—the Sadducees do not believe in immortality, and it seems their personal beliefs are literally grounded in an earthly image of heaven. Jesus responds by dealing with the fact of the resurrection. Jesus quotes Exodus 3:6, where God identifies himself as the "God of Abraham" and tells them that God is a living God of a living people. This is fulfilled by his own resurrection on Easter Day.

Denying the Resurrection and believing in a philosophy of pleasurable life can lead to an inability to recognize the sinful life. In some extreme situations, such as with the Taliban, the pursuit of the pleasurable life and possible rewards in paradise could lead to sin and suicide bombings.

The purpose of God's law is simply that we love God and all created beings. God is love and everything God does flows from this love for all. God loved us first, and our love for God is our response to God's exceeding grace and kindness toward us. Believing in Resurrection can lead to a transformed life in this world.

The Rev. Riaz Mubarak
Vicar of St. Luke's Church
Abbottabad, Pakistan

Questions

Like Sadducees who believed in their own reasons and philosophy, how might you check your beliefs by matching your understanding with the Word of God? Is this understanding divinely or humanly based?

Prayer

Lord, your love surpasses all. Fill our hearts with your love and make them overflow to reach others, sharing with them the simple faith of love and understanding. Amen.

Matthew 23:1-22

23 Then Jesus said to the crowds and to his disciples, 2"The scribes and the Pharisees sit on Moses' seat; 3therefore, do whatever they teach you and follow it; but do not do as they do, for they do not practice what they teach. 4They tie up heavy burdens, hard to bear, and lay them on the shoulders of others; but they themselves are unwilling to lift a finger to move them. 5They do all their deeds to be seen by others; for they make their phylacteries broad and their fringes long. 6They love to have the place of honor at banquets and the best seats in the synagogues, 7and to be greeted with respect in the marketplaces, and to have people call them rabbi. 8But you are not to be called rabbi, for you have one teacher, and you are all students. 9And call no one your father on earth, for you have one Father—the one in heaven. 10Nor are you to be called instructors, for you have one instructor, the Messiah. 11The greatest among you will be your servant. 12All who exalt themselves will be humbled, and all who humble themselves will be exalted.

13"But woe to you, scribes and Pharisees, hypocrites! For you lock people out of the kingdom of heaven. For you do not go in yourselves, and when others are going in, you stop them. 15Woe to you, scribes and Pharisees, hypocrites! For you cross sea and land to make a single convert, and you make the new convert twice as much a child of hell as yourselves. 16Woe to you, blind guides, who say, 'Whoever swears by the sanctuary is bound by nothing, but whoever swears by the gold of the sanctuary is bound by the oath.' ¹⁷You blind fools! For which is greater, the gold or the sanctuary that has made the gold sacred? ¹⁸And you say, 'Whoever swears by the altar is bound by nothing, but whoever swears by the gift that is on the altar is bound by the oath.' ¹⁹How blind you are! For which is greater, the gift or the altar that makes the gift sacred? ²⁰So whoever swears by the altar, swears by it and by everything on it; ²¹and whoever swears by the sanctuary, swears by it and by the one who dwells in it; ²²and whoever swears by heaven, swears by the throne of God and by the one who is seated upon it."

Reflection

Walking through Peshawar with a friend, we heard an imam teaching his students in a Madrassa. He told them "the Christians, Shias, and Hindus are infidels, and as Muslims, we need to take a step of Jihad against them. Don't shake hands with them and don't eat with them." My Christian friend, upon hearing these words, became angry and spoke out against him. This caught the attention of some passersby, and they stopped to listen. My friend challenged the teaching of the imam, saying that it was hatred and nonsense.

However, the imam justified his remarks by pointing to certain verses from the Quran. My friend continued: "You are making these innocents into enemies rather than good men." Some men threatened him and even me. I took my friend away hurriedly to avoid further religious conflict.

In this passage, Jesus admonishes the scribes and Pharisees for their pretentious practices. In their misguided zeal for religion, they seek respect and honor for themselves rather than for God and for God's word. They make the practice of their faith a burden rather than a joy for the people they are supposed to serve. It is for this reason that Jesus issues such a stern rebuke. Jesus gives a series of examples to show how misguided they are. They are leading people to Pharisaism rather than to God.

Jesus also chastises them for their evasion of binding oaths and solemn promises. Oaths made to God are considered binding, but the Pharisees find clever ways to evade their obligations. Through their own pride and prejudice they blindly shut the door of their own hearts and minds to understanding God's kingdom.

The Rev. Riaz Mubarak
Vicar of St. Luke's Church
Abbottabad, Pakistan

Question

How do we show the people of this world love, peace, and good fellowship?

Prayer

Heavenly Father, your Word is life for us. May we not shut the doors to the kingdom of heaven through disbelief, indifference, or disobedience. Help us to listen to your voice and to transform our lives more fully to your word. Amen.

Matthew 23:23-39

²³"Woe to you, scribes and Pharisees, hypocrites! For you tithe mint, dill, and cumin, and have neglected the weightier matters of the law: justice and mercy and faith. It is these you ought to have practiced without neglecting the others. ²⁴You blind guides! You strain out a gnat but swallow a camel! ²⁵Woe to you, scribes and Pharisees, hypocrites! For you clean the outside of the cup and of the plate, but inside they are full of greed and self-indulgence. ²⁶You blind Pharisee! First clean the inside of the cup, so that the outside also may become clean. ²⁷Woe to you, scribes and Pharisees, hypocrites! For you are like whitewashed tombs, which on the outside look beautiful, but inside they are full of the bones of the dead and of all kinds of filth. ²⁸So you also on the outside look righteous to others, but inside you are full of hypocrisy and lawlessness. ²⁹Woe to you, scribes and Pharisees, hypocrites! For you build the tombs of the prophets and decorate the graves of the righteous, ³⁰and you say, 'If we had lived in the days of our ancestors, we would not have taken part with them in shedding the blood of the prophets.' ³¹Thus you testify against yourselves that you are descendants of those who murdered the prophets. ³²Fill up, then, the measure of your ancestors. ³³You snakes, you brood of vipers! How can you escape being sentenced to hell?

³⁴"Therefore I send you prophets, sages, and scribes, some of whom you will kill and crucify, and some you will flog in your synagogues and pursue

from town to town, ³⁵so that upon you may come all the righteous blood shed on earth, from the blood of righteous Abel to the blood of Zechariah son of Barachiah, whom you murdered between the sanctuary and the altar. ³⁶Truly I tell you, all this will come upon this generation. ³⁷"Jerusalem, Jerusalem, the city that kills the prophets and stones those who are sent to it! How often have I desired to gather your children together as a hen gathers her brood under her wings, and you were not willing! ³⁸See, your house is left to you, desolate. ³⁹For I tell you, you will not see me again until you say, 'Blessed is the one who comes in the name of the Lord.'"

Reflection

Today's reading presents some of the harshest words attributed by Matthew to Jesus, words that have fostered tensions, antagonism, and misunderstandings between Christians and Jews over the centuries. Contemporary scholars suggest that "the seven woes against the scribes and Pharisees," which are unique to Matthew's Gospel, may provide a glimpse into the tensions that really existed between Jesus' followers and other Jewish sects in the late first century.

In particularly harsh and judgmental words, Jesus, standing in the temple, accuses his rivals of being hypocrites, blind guides, snakes, a brood of vipers. They tithe their monetary treasure while neglecting to practice justice, mercy, and faith. They outwardly appear pious and righteous while inwardly they are unclean and impure. They lock people out of the kingdom of heaven through their own blindness to God's way.

This is a fire-and-brimstone sermon, and like a good preacher, Jesus concludes with an expression of love and compassion for God's hurting world and aching people, and then exits with a final dismissal of the temple as a place of desolation. It shouldn't come as a surprise that this text is not included in the Sunday lectionary.

What are we to make of these words of woe in our own context? Frankly, I think they are a good warning to the church, the body of the Risen Christ. If we are willing and able to follow Jesus' advice and take the log out of our own eye, then Matthew's condemnation of the scribes and the Pharisees can be a mirror for us.

The Very Rev. Tracey Lind
Dean of Trinity Cathedral
Cleveland, Ohio

Questions

How do you act like a hypocrite, and what might you do to change your behavior?

How are you judgmental, and how might you change your attitude?

Prayer

We confess to you, Lord, all our past unfaithfulness: the pride, hypocrisy, and impatience of our lives...Accept our repentance, Lord,...for all false judgments, for uncharitable thoughts toward our neighbors, and for our prejudice and contempt toward those who differ from us. Amen.

—The Book of Common Prayer, p. 268

Matthew 24:1-22

24 As Jesus came out of the temple and was going away, his disciples came to point out to him the buildings of the temple. ²Then he asked them, "You see all these, do you not? Truly I tell you, not one stone will be left here upon another; all will be thrown down." ³When he was sitting on the Mount of Olives, the disciples came to him privately, saying, "Tell us, when will this be, and what will be the sign of your coming and of the end of the age?"

⁴Jesus answered them, "Beware that no one leads you astray. ⁵For many will come in my name, saying, 'I am the Messiah!' and they will lead many astray. ⁶And you will hear of wars and rumors of wars; see that you are not alarmed; for this must take place, but the end is not yet. ⁷For nation will rise against nation, and kingdom against kingdom, and there will be famines and earthquakes in various places: ⁸all this is but the beginning of the birthpangs. ⁹Then they will hand you over to be tortured and will put you to death, and you will be hated by all nations because of my name. ¹⁰Then many will fall away, and they will betray one another and hate one another. ¹¹And many false prophets will arise and lead many astray. ¹²And because of the increase of lawlessness, the love of many will grow cold. ¹³But the one who endures to the end will be saved. ¹⁴And this good news of the kingdom will be proclaimed throughout the world, as a testimony to all the nations; and then the end will come. ¹⁵So when you see the desolating sacrilege standing in the holy place, as was spoken

of by the prophet Daniel (let the reader understand), [16]then those in Judea must flee to the mountains; [17]the one on the housetop must not go down to take what is in the house; [18]the one in the field must not turn back to get a coat. [19]Woe to those who are pregnant and to those who are nursing infants in those days! [20]Pray that your flight may not be in winter or on a sabbath. [21]For at that time there will be great suffering, such as has not been from the beginning of the world until now, no, and never will be. [22]And if those days had not been cut short, no one would be saved; but for the sake of the elect those days will be cut short."

Reflection

Today's reading recalls what probably happened in the fall of Jerusalem in 70 C.E. when, according to the Jewish historian Josephus, more than 1.1 million people perished. This siege of Jerusalem was among the most grueling in all of human history, and the destruction of the Temple was complete, causing a fire that could be seen for miles. Before the attack on the holy city, there was insurrection and rebellion in Judea and infighting among the imperial leadership of Rome. During and after the fall of Jerusalem, there was famine and plague throughout the land. History even records an earthquake of sizable proportion in the latter half of the first century. But, the Son of Man did not return in power and great glory.

Jesus' predictions of apocalypse actually have come true over and over again. During the past two millennia, many great temples and cathedrals have been destroyed by the powers of war, revolution, and terrorism, and the world has experienced a variety of plagues and natural disasters. Most generations have been able to say, "Surely, this is what Jesus was talking about—this must be the end." And still, the Son of Man has not returned in power and glory.

Today, the end is still not here, and yet, we are called to believe. Our work as Christians in the trials and tribulations of this world is not to abandon the faith but rather enliven it, trusting in God, the one who is certain and whose promises will not fail.

The Very Rev. Tracey Lind
Dean of Trinity Cathedral
Cleveland, Ohio

Questions _____

Who is experiencing trials and tribulations and needs your prayer and action?

How are you working for peace and justice in your daily life?

Prayer _____

Gracious God, watch over those who live with war and insurrection, famine and disease, injustice and terror. Protect, guide, and bless them. Help us to work for justice and peace. Amen.

Matthew 24:23-41

²³"Then if anyone says to you, 'Look! Here is the Messiah!' or 'There he is!' —do not believe it. ²⁴For false messiahs and false prophets will appear and produce great signs and omens, to lead astray, if possible, even the elect. ²⁵Take note, I have told you beforehand. ²⁶So, if they say to you, 'Look! He is in the wilderness,' do not go out. If they say, 'Look! He is in the inner rooms,' do not believe it. ²⁷For as the lightning comes from the east and flashes as far as the west, so will be the coming of the Son of Man. ²⁸Wherever the corpse is, there the vultures will gather. ²⁹Immediately after the suffering of those days the sun will be darkened, and the moon will not give its light; the stars will fall from heaven, and the powers of heaven will be shaken. ³⁰Then the sign of the Son of Man will appear in heaven, and then all the tribes of the earth will mourn, and they will see 'the Son of Man coming on the clouds of heaven' with power and great glory. ³¹And he will send out his angels with a loud trumpet call, and they will gather his elect from the four winds, from one end of heaven to the other.

³²"From the fig tree learn its lesson: as soon as its branch becomes tender and puts forth its leaves, you know that summer is near. ³³So also, when you see all these things, you know that he is near, at the very gates. ³⁴Truly I tell you, this generation will not pass away until all these things have taken place. ³⁵Heaven and earth will pass away, but my words will not pass away. ³⁶But about that day and hour no one knows,

neither the angels of heaven, nor the Son, but only the Father. [37]For as the days of Noah were, so will be the coming of the Son of Man. [38]For as in those days before the flood they were eating and drinking, marrying and giving in marriage, until the day Noah entered the ark, [39]and they knew nothing until the flood came and swept them all away, so too will be the coming of the Son of Man. [40]Then two will be in the field; one will be taken and one will be left. [41]Two women will be grinding meal together; one will be taken and one will be left."

Reflection

Jesus teaches the disciples about the events that will signal the decisive coming of God to make things right and to gather together the people of God. The advice pummels and buffets, ricocheting back and forth between warning and assurance. First: don't expect reliable counsel from other people—be suspicious of those who claim they know. Next: it's about as predictable as a bolt of lightning. Then: there's no way you could miss the event when the Son of Man comes on clouds descending. Actually: the shoots on the fig tree at the edge of summer, so fragile, will hint that God is near. Finally: No one knows except the Father; people will have no warning at all; and the taking and leaving will be arbitrary and divisive. In the midst of daily work at farm or hearth, companions will be torn asunder.

Christian imagination about the end times has its source in the experience of suffering. Jesus' followers and those in the community of Matthew's Gospel know poverty, violence, and persecution. Their vision of God's intervention with cosmic powers acts to motivate and sustain them in the face of injustice. Throughout history, some Christian groups, from a position of social power, have used these scriptural visions to name others as enemies or to evade responsibility for justice and peace in the present. Jesus' words undercut claims to interpretive certainty and direct us to acute attention and renewed faithfulness.

The Very Rev. Cynthia Briggs Kittredge
Dean and President of Seminary of the Southwest
Austin, Texas

A Journey with Matthew

Questions

How do you and your community of faith imagine the coming of the Son of Man?

How does your anticipation change how you live in the present?

Prayer

God of power and great glory, help us accept our not knowing. Do not let us be led astray. Amen.

Matthew 24:42—25:13

⁴²"Keep awake therefore, for you do not know on what day your Lord is coming. ⁴³But understand this: if the owner of the house had known in what part of the night the thief was coming, he would have stayed awake and would not have let his house be broken into. ⁴⁴Therefore you also must be ready, for the Son of Man is coming at an unexpected hour. ⁴⁵Who then is the faithful and wise slave, whom his master has put in charge of his household, to give the other slaves their allowance of food at the proper time? ⁴⁶Blessed is that slave whom his master will find at work when he arrives. ⁴⁷Truly I tell you, he will put that one in charge of all his possessions. ⁴⁸But if that wicked slave says to himself, 'My master is delayed,' ⁴⁹and he begins to beat his fellow slaves, and eats and drinks with drunkards, ⁵⁰the master of that slave will come on a day when he does not expect him and at an hour that he does not know. ⁵¹He will cut him in pieces and put him with the hypocrites, where there will be weeping and gnashing of teeth.

25 "Then the kingdom of heaven will be like this. Ten bridesmaids took their lamps and went to meet the bridegroom. ²Five of them were foolish, and five were wise. ³When the foolish took their lamps, they took no oil with them; ⁴but the wise took flasks of oil with their lamps. ⁵As the bridegroom was delayed, all of them became drowsy and slept. ⁶But at midnight there was a shout, 'Look! Here is the bridegroom! Come out

to meet him.' [7]Then all those bridesmaids got up and trimmed their lamps. [8]The foolish said to the wise, 'Give us some of your oil, for our lamps are going out.' [9]But the wise replied, 'No! there will not be enough for you and for us; you had better go to the dealers and buy some for yourselves.' [10]And while they went to buy it, the bridegroom came, and those who were ready went with him into the wedding banquet; and the door was shut. [11]Later the other bridesmaids came also, saying, 'Lord, lord, open to us.' [12]But he replied, 'Truly I tell you, I do not know you.' [13]Keep awake therefore, for you know neither the day nor the hour."

Reflection

Three parables of increasing length and complexity play with the imagery of staying awake and being ready. All involve the unexpected arrival—of a burglar, of a master, of a bridegroom. Two take place at night—the first in the threatening and strangely criminal comparison with a housebreaking and the coming of a thief in the night—and the third with the joyful public occasion of a wedding. In these parables, the natural nighttime activity of sleeping is negative, because in the first, the unconscious one will be robbed, and in the third, the sleeper will miss the feast. In the second parable, the unwise slave, believing that the master will not return soon, figuratively sleeps by carousing and beating his fellow slaves. All three warn in severe language of the consequences of falling asleep: being robbed, being hacked to death, and being shut out.

Parables of retribution reflect the harsh social world of the first century and in many ways resemble features of ours as well. The shock they evoke is a means to motivate the Christian to right action and spiritual alertness.

There is a classic nightmare in which you are unprepared, improperly dressed, and too late for some sort of public presentation. The predicament of the foolish bridesmaids arouses the extreme shame and fear of those critical moments—it sharpens our sympathy for the drowsy, undersupplied attendants who failed at their duty and lost their chance to meet the bridegroom and to be welcomed into the warm interior of the banquet. How much happier to be counted among the wise, who made ready the fuel to burn and to illumine their long, long wait?

The Very Rev. Cynthia Briggs Kittredge
Dean and President of Seminary of the Southwest
Austin, Texas

A Journey with Matthew

Questions

How do you make sense of the violent language of judgment attributed to God in the Gospel of Matthew?

What supplies are required to be ready to respond to the coming of God?

Prayer

Holy and loving God, have mercy when we are foolish, when we mistreat others, when we are ignorant and oblivious of danger. Help us to be wakeful and wise. Amen.

Matthew 25:14-30

[14]"For it is as if a man, going on a journey, summoned his slaves and entrusted his property to them; [15]to one he gave five talents, to another two, to another one, to each according to his ability. Then he went away. [16]The one who had received the five talents went off at once and traded with them, and made five more talents. [17]In the same way, the one who had the two talents made two more talents. [18]But the one who had received the one talent went off and dug a hole in the ground and hid his master's money. [19]After a long time the master of those slaves came and settled accounts with them. [20]Then the one who had received the five talents came forward, bringing five more talents, saying, 'Master, you handed over to me five talents; see, I have made five more talents.' [21]His master said to him, 'Well done, good and trustworthy slave; you have been trustworthy in a few things, I will put you in charge of many things; enter into the joy of your master.' [22]And the one with the two talents also came forward, saying, 'Master, you handed over to me two talents; see, I have made two more talents.' [23]His master said to him, 'Well done, good and trustworthy slave; you have been trustworthy in a few things, I will put you in charge of many things; enter into the joy of your master.' [24]Then the one who had received the one talent also came forward, saying, 'Master, I knew that you were a harsh man, reaping where you did not sow, and gathering where you did not scatter seed; [25]so I was afraid, and I went and hid

your talent in the ground. Here you have what is yours.' [26]But his master replied, 'You wicked and lazy slave! You knew, did you, that I reap where I did not sow, and gather where I did not scatter? [27]Then you ought to have invested my money with the bankers, and on my return I would have received what was my own with interest. [28]So take the talent from him, and give it to the one with the ten talents. [29]For to all those who have, more will be given, and they will have an abundance; but from those who have nothing, even what they have will be taken away. [30]As for this worthless slave, throw him into the outer darkness, where there will be weeping and gnashing of teeth.' "

Reflection

The parable of the talents is classic parable. It tells us three things. First, resources are not evenly divided. Some people receive more than others, whether they are more intelligent, have more talents or benefit from better parenting, coaching, and teaching. Life is not fair. What matters is what we do with what we have been given, not how much we have received.

Second, there is accountability. We live in an unaccountable culture. "I'm not responsible for failing the test. It was my parent's fault for not making me study more, my brother's fault for distracting me, and my teacher's fault for not teaching well. I'm not to blame." Our culture increasingly functions like this. Criminals are not at fault. Society drove them to crime. No one wants to take responsibility. God, however, expects us to be accountable for our actions.

Third, there is judgment. Just as we do not like accountability, we dislike judgment. At times, the Church has overdone judgment, but judgment is part of accountability. In the parable, the owner returns to judge how each of his stewards used what was entrusted to him. To those who have exercised their talents wisely, he distributes more. To the one who wasted his talent, he removes his talent and gives it to others who will use it wisely.

Talents are meant to be used for others. If we hoard them and use them solely for ourselves, God will not increase our talents. But if we use gifts and talents to bless others and to serve Jesus, God, like a wise investor, will increase our gifts so that the kingdom of heaven can flourish.

The Rev. Marek P. Zabriskie
Founder of the Center for Biblical Studies
Rector of St. Thomas Church, Whitemarsh
Fort Washington, Pennsylvania

Questions

What gifts do you hide that God longs for you to share with others and use to serve Jesus?

In what ways do you resist being held accountable by others and by God?

Prayer

Gracious God, what matters is not how many talents we have been given, but how we use them. Help us to use our gifts wisely to serve you and others, entrusting that you will multiply our talents when we wisely put them to use. In Jesus' name we pray. Amen.

Matthew 25:31-46

[31]"When the Son of Man comes in his glory, and all the angels with him, then he will sit on the throne of his glory. [32]All the nations will be gathered before him, and he will separate people one from another as a shepherd separates the sheep from the goats, [33]and he will put the sheep at his right hand and the goats at the left. [34]Then the king will say to those at his right hand, 'Come, you that are blessed by my Father, inherit the kingdom prepared for you from the foundation of the world; [35]for I was hungry and you gave me food, I was thirsty and you gave me something to drink, I was a stranger and you welcomed me, [36]I was naked and you gave me clothing, I was sick and you took care of me, I was in prison and you visited me.' [37]Then the righteous will answer him, 'Lord, when was it that we saw you hungry and gave you food, or thirsty and gave you something to drink? [38]And when was it that we saw you a stranger and welcomed you, or naked and gave you clothing? [39]And when was it that we saw you sick or in prison and visited you?' [40]And the king will answer them, 'Truly I tell you, just as you did it to one of the least of these who are members of my family, you did it to me.' [41]Then he will say to those at his left hand, 'You that are accursed, depart from me into the eternal fire prepared for the devil and his angels; [42]for I was hungry and you gave me no food, I was thirsty and you gave me nothing to drink, [43]I was a stranger and you did not welcome me, naked and you did not give me clothing, sick and in prison and you did not visit me.' [44]Then they also will

answer, 'Lord, when was it that we saw you hungry or thirsty or a stranger or naked or sick or in prison, and did not take care of you?' [45]Then he will answer them, 'Truly I tell you, just as you did not do it to one of the least of these, you did not do it to me.' [46]And these will go away into eternal punishment, but the righteous into eternal life."

Reflection

This is one of the most classic passages in the Bible. Jesus says that when the Messiah comes in glory, he will separate the sheep from the goats. Episcopalians are notorious for disliking judgment, but God and the Church have high expectations for us.

If you have any doubt, reread The Episcopal Church's Baptismal Covenant found in *The Book of Common Prayer* (pp. 304-305). "Will you continue in the apostles' teaching…persevere in resisting evil…proclaim by word and example the Good News of God in Christ…seek and serve Christ in all persons…strive for justice and peace among all people…?" These are high expectations!

Jesus tells us that the "king" (or God) will say, "for I was hungry and you gave me food, I was thirsty and you gave me something to drink, I was a stranger and you welcomed me, I was naked and you gave me clothing, I was sick and you took care of me, I was in prison and you visited me" (25:35-36). His listeners will ask when this occurred.

"Truly, I tell you, just as you did it to one of the least of these who are members of my family, you did it to me," notes the king (25:40). We may never directly provide Jesus with a warm coat, a comfortable bed, a good meal, or visit him in prison, but if we do this for anyone in need, we will have done it for Jesus.

We encounter Christ whenever we serve those who are poor and needy, whether they live in poverty or are a neighbor or family member facing challenges. Whatever we do for the least of these, we will do for Jesus.

The Rev. Marek P. Zabriskie
Founder of the Center for Biblical Studies
Rector of St. Thomas Church, Whitemarsh
Fort Washington, Pennsylvania

Questions

In what ways do you care for the lowly and the oppressed?

As you helped another person, have you ever felt as if you were helping Jesus himself?

Prayer

Almighty God, you long for us to be your hands and feet, reaching out to care for the poor and needy. Help us to discover your presence as we assist those who are afflicted or who are on the margins of society and long for your healing and compassion. In Jesus' name we pray. Amen.

Matthew 26:1-16

26 When Jesus had finished saying all these things, he said to his disciples, ²"You know that after two days the Passover is coming, and the Son of Man will be handed over to be crucified." ³Then the chief priests and the elders of the people gathered in the palace of the high priest, who was called Caiaphas, ⁴and they conspired to arrest Jesus by stealth and kill him. ⁵But they said, "Not during the festival, or there may be a riot among the people."

⁶Now while Jesus was at Bethany in the house of Simon the leper, ⁷a woman came to him with an alabaster jar of very costly ointment, and she poured it on his head as he sat at the table. ⁸But when the disciples saw it, they were angry and said, "Why this waste? ⁹For this ointment could have been sold for a large sum, and the money given to the poor." ¹⁰But Jesus, aware of this, said to them, "Why do you trouble the woman? She has performed a good service for me. ¹¹For you always have the poor with you, but you will not always have me. ¹²By pouring this ointment on my body she has prepared me for burial. ¹³Truly I tell you, wherever this good news is proclaimed in the whole world, what she has done will be told in remembrance of her."

¹⁴Then one of the twelve, who was called Judas Iscariot, went to the chief priests ¹⁵and said, "What will you give me if I betray him to you?" They paid him thirty pieces of silver. ¹⁶And from that moment he began to look for an opportunity to betray him.

Reflection

As the storm clouds gather and Jesus knows he is entering the last hours of his life, what are we to make of this quick passage, this anecdote from Matthew that briefly alights before quickly taking us somewhere else?

The uneasy relationship between the Christian and money is brought into stark relief here: is Jesus counseling his followers that there is no point in almsgiving, because the recipients are still poor after the gift?

Hardly. In his constant exhortations to his friends and followers to reexamine their assumptions about money and how it operates in our lives, Jesus does not simply recommend that everyone he meets divest themselves of all their goods and head into the wilderness. His scorn is not for wealth but for money that grows beyond its legitimate boundaries to take up too much room in our lives. Figure out what's really important! Even more crucially, figure out what's really important to you, and challenge that thing's place in your life.

Scripture delights in the enjoyment of plenty, using terms immediately recognized by a hardscrabble people scratching out a daily living in the eastern Mediterranean...overflowing oil, a pressed-down measure, nets filled with writhing fish, a land that flows with milk and honey.

In this moment of intimacy and comfort, washed, perfumed, anointed, a man of the dusty street is contemplating the end of his short life. He is preparing himself inwardly, and in a moment of rare physical comfort, reminds his friends, in effect, "Lighten up, and keep your eyes on what's important. Don't count the cost of every moment. Instead, concentrate on the whole picture."

Ray Suarez
Journalist and Host of *Inside Story*
Washington, D.C.

Questions

Jesus' words are challenging: "For you always have the poor with you, but you will not always have me." Is he counseling a kind of self-indulgence?

What does the juxtaposition of Jesus' rejection of selling the ointment for money and Judas' striking a bargain with the priests tell you about God's economy?

Prayer

Dearest Lord Jesus, grant us the grace of physical comfort in the midst of our labor and the challenges of our life. Let those small moments remind us of the gift of our senses, and the joy of Creation. Amen.

Matthew 26:17-35

[17]On the first day of Unleavened Bread the disciples came to Jesus, saying, "Where do you want us to make the preparations for you to eat the Passover?" [18]He said, "Go into the city to a certain man, and say to him, 'The Teacher says, My time is near; I will keep the Passover at your house with my disciples.'" [19]So the disciples did as Jesus had directed them, and they prepared the Passover meal. [20]When it was evening, he took his place with the twelve; [21]and while they were eating, he said, "Truly I tell you, one of you will betray me." [22]And they became greatly distressed and began to say to him one after another, "Surely not I, Lord?" [23]He answered, "The one who has dipped his hand into the bowl with me will betray me. [24]The Son of Man goes as it is written of him, but woe to that one by whom the Son of Man is betrayed! It would have been better for that one not to have been born." [25]Judas, who betrayed him, said, "Surely not I, Rabbi?" He replied, "You have said so."

[26]While they were eating, Jesus took a loaf of bread, and after blessing it he broke it, gave it to the disciples, and said, "Take, eat; this is my body." [27]Then he took a cup, and after giving thanks he gave it to them, saying, "Drink from it, all of you; [28]for this is my blood of the covenant, which is poured out for many for the forgiveness of sins. [29]I tell you, I will never again drink of this fruit of the vine until that day when I drink it new with you in my Father's kingdom." [30]When they had sung the hymn, they went out to the Mount of Olives.

[31]Then Jesus said to them, "You will all become deserters because of me this night; for it is written, 'I will strike the shepherd, and the sheep of the flock will be scattered.' [32]But after I am raised up, I will go ahead of you to Galilee." [33]Peter said to him, "Though all become deserters because of you, I will never desert you." [34]Jesus said to him, "Truly I tell you, this very night, before the cock crows, you will deny me three times." [35]Peter said to him, "Even though I must die with you, I will not deny you." And so said all the disciples.

Reflection

Here we see Jesus, in what would be the last week of his life, swept along by events, and yet in control of them at the same time. Even as the hours dwindle, he calmly prepares for the Passover with his friends and begins to let them in on what he knows is about to transpire.

One will betray him into the hands of his executioners.

Another will deny even knowing him.

With the weakness and fear of men who had shared so much with him staring him in the face, Jesus does not waver. He heads to the Passover, a celebration of the deliverance and survival of his people, the Jewish people, to celebrate and begin to say goodbye.

Human, divine, human, divine. Jesus shows us both aspects of his character in these tense hours. Unlike any man, he is able to see what's coming, and yet like any man he faces the dread of suffering and taking leave of his beloved friends.

We're in the Upper Room. As human beings we are seized by the same mix of emotions descending on the people at the table: denial, resistance, fear, weakness, defiance.

As this stunning drama plays out, nothing less than the central sacrament of the church is spoken out loud for the first time, words that echo from that moment on down two thousand years of history. Throughout scripture, the moments when God and humankind are unusually close are punctuated by reassurance, "Don't be afraid." In this intimate, simple moment in Matthew, Jesus does the same, telling the people closest to him during his ministry on earth that he will always be with them, every time they break bread, drink, and give thanks for what they have.

Ray Suarez
Journalist and Host of *Inside Story*
Washington, D.C.

Questions

Are you prepared to accept the assurance that even when you desert Jesus, he has promised never to desert you?

Is the shame of denying Jesus the end of the story? Does this story in Matthew allow a path back to being faithful, and, if we're lucky, fearless?

Prayer

Dear Lord Jesus, we thank you for the gift of Eucharist. May it always be to us, your flock, a time of gratitude, strength, renewal, and joy, until the day you promised, when we share it with you in your Father's kingdom. Amen.

Matthew 26:36-56

³⁶Then Jesus went with them to a place called Gethsemane; and he said to his disciples, "Sit here while I go over there and pray." ³⁷He took with him Peter and the two sons of Zebedee, and began to be grieved and agitated. ³⁸Then he said to them, "I am deeply grieved, even to death; remain here, and stay awake with me." ³⁹And going a little farther, he threw himself on the ground and prayed, "My Father, if it is possible, let this cup pass from me; yet not what I want but what you want." ⁴⁰Then he came to the disciples and found them sleeping; and he said to Peter, "So, could you not stay awake with me one hour? ⁴¹Stay awake and pray that you may not come into the time of trial; the spirit indeed is willing, but the flesh is weak." ⁴²Again he went away for the second time and prayed, "My Father, if this cannot pass unless I drink it, your will be done." ⁴³Again he came and found them sleeping, for their eyes were heavy. ⁴⁴So leaving them again, he went away and prayed for the third time, saying the same words. ⁴⁵Then he came to the disciples and said to them, "Are you still sleeping and taking your rest? See, the hour is at hand, and the Son of Man is betrayed into the hands of sinners. ⁴⁶Get up, let us be going. See, my betrayer is at hand."

⁴⁷While he was still speaking, Judas, one of the twelve, arrived; with him was a large crowd with swords and clubs, from the chief priests and the elders of the people. ⁴⁸Now the betrayer had given them a sign, saying,

"The one I will kiss is the man; arrest him." ⁴⁹At once he came up to Jesus and said, "Greetings, Rabbi!" and kissed him. ⁵⁰Jesus said to him, "Friend, do what you are here to do." Then they came and laid hands on Jesus and arrested him. ⁵¹Suddenly, one of those with Jesus put his hand on his sword, drew it, and struck the slave of the high priest, cutting off his ear. ⁵²Then Jesus said to him, "Put your sword back into its place; for all who take the sword will perish by the sword. ⁵³Do you think that I cannot appeal to my Father, and he will at once send me more than twelve legions of angels? ⁵⁴But how then would the scriptures be fulfilled, which say it must happen in this way?" ⁵⁵At that hour Jesus said to the crowds, "Have you come out with swords and clubs to arrest me as though I were a bandit? Day after day I sat in the temple teaching, and you did not arrest me. ⁵⁶But all this has taken place, so that the scriptures of the prophets may be fulfilled." Then all the disciples deserted him and fled.

Reflection

Notice the change in Jesus' mood when the armed mob arrives—his grief and agitation are gone, and he takes charge immediately. In the company of his nearest and dearest, he let his vulnerability show, but not now: he is again the bold Jesus his followers expect him to be, confident in his own power and firm in his resolve to lay it down.

We expect this of our Jesus, too. A number of heresies in the earliest years of the Church's existence simply couldn't come to terms with Jesus' humanity. Early followers couldn't wrap their minds around a God who was willing to know fear like our fear, pain like our pain, disappointment like the disappointment we know. Some of them theorized that Jesus was just pretending to be afraid. Some suggested that his pain was not real. Some even thought that his body was not real! Others went the other way, teaching that the fact of his suffering meant he could not have been divine.

Much ink and some blood was spilled in argumentation about how it was that Jesus was the Christ. So many centuries later, we still cannot codify just how it was that Jesus was who he was. It is, we say in the end, a mystery.

Let's not lose sleep over imponderables. It is the story of the Passion that matters here, the oldest story in the New Testament, a story first told with no reference to theological hairsplitting about the Trinity. Now it begins.

The Rev. Barbara Cawthorne Crafton
Author and Retreat Leader
Newark, New Jersey

Questions _____

How do you respond to the idea of Jesus being afraid?

"Truly human and truly divine" is how we describe Jesus—and human beings learn primarily from their mistakes. Do you think that Jesus knew everything?

What would it mean to you if he did not?

Prayer _____

Lord Jesus Christ, you prayed in the Garden of Gethsemane to be delivered from death, and you went on to die. We will do the same. We give you thanks for showing us that our own fears do not draw God's love away from us, and we ask you to show yourself to us at the end of our own life on earth. This we pray in your own most Holy Name. Amen.

Matthew 26:57-75

57Those who had arrested Jesus took him to Caiaphas the high priest, in whose house the scribes and the elders had gathered. 58But Peter was following him at a distance, as far as the courtyard of the high priest; and going inside, he sat with the guards in order to see how this would end. 59Now the chief priests and the whole council were looking for false testimony against Jesus so that they might put him to death, 60but they found none, though many false witnesses came forward. At last two came forward 61and said, "This fellow said, 'I am able to destroy the temple of God and to build it in three days.'" 62The high priest stood up and said, "Have you no answer? What is it that they testify against you?" 63But Jesus was silent. Then the high priest said to him, "I put you under oath before the living God, tell us if you are the Messiah, the Son of God." 64Jesus said to him, "You have said so. But I tell you, from now on you will see the Son of Man seated at the right hand of Power and coming on the clouds of heaven." 65Then the high priest tore his clothes and said, "He has blasphemed! Why do we still need witnesses? You have now heard his blasphemy. 66What is your verdict?" They answered, "He deserves death." 67Then they spat in his face and struck him; and some slapped him, 68saying, "Prophesy to us, you Messiah! Who is it that struck you?"

69Now Peter was sitting outside in the courtyard. A servant-girl came to him and said, "You also were with Jesus the Galilean." 70But he denied it before all of them, saying, "I do not know what you are talking about." ⁷¹When he went out to the porch, another servant-girl saw him, and she said to the bystanders, "This man was with Jesus of Nazareth." ⁷²Again he denied it with an oath, "I do not know the man." ⁷³After a little while the bystanders came up and said to Peter, "Certainly you are also one of them, for your accent betrays you." ⁷⁴Then he began to curse, and he swore an oath, "I do not know the man!" At that moment the cock crowed. ⁷⁵Then Peter remembered what Jesus had said: "Before the cock crows, you will deny me three times." And he went out and wept bitterly.

Reflection

This must be the lowest moment of Peter's life. After so loudly proclaiming that he would be faithful to his leader no matter what, he folds immediately. All his bravery is hypothetical; when challenged for real, it fails. Matthew tells us that Peter goes out and weeps bitterly when he hears the rooster herald the dawn on the day Jesus is to die…and we can feel his shame from two thousand years away.

Think back. All of us have had a moment like this, a time when we failed to do the good we intended and did something else instead. Maybe it was something big, like Peter's failure of nerve, or maybe it was an honest mistake, with terrible consequences. But we all know what it is to have been less than we ought to have been. To wish with all our hearts, after the fact, that we had not done what we did.

Peter is the rock upon which the Church is built, we know. Jesus gives him this name: "Petrus" (in Syriac, "Cephas") means "rock." Strong and immovable, he would be—but Peter is nothing of the kind, not in this passage and not in many others describing his actions before the resurrection. Though he wields great authority in the earliest Christian community, the gospel writers do not seek to hide his shortcomings.

What can it mean, their remarkable candor, if not that Peter's failures did not define him? And that our failures do not define us?

The Rev. Barbara Cawthorne Crafton
Author and Retreat Leader
Newark, New Jersey

A Journey with Matthew

Questions

The news is full of scandals involving leaders. We've gotten used to hearing them deny their guilt until the facts catch up with them, and sometimes even after that. Does such a failure disqualify a leader? Why or why not?

Prayer

Lord Christ, your friend Peter denied you out of fear, and yet he became the leader of the first Christian community. Help us to see our own failures as chances to begin again and not as a measure of our worth, for you have made us worthy in your eyes. For this and all your mercies, we give you hearty thanks. Amen.

Matthew 27:1-23

27 When morning came, all the chief priests and the elders of the people conferred together against Jesus in order to bring about his death. ²They bound him, led him away, and handed him over to Pilate the governor. ³When Judas, his betrayer, saw that Jesus was condemned, he repented and brought back the thirty pieces of silver to the chief priests and the elders. ⁴He said, "I have sinned by betraying innocent blood." But they said, "What is that to us? See to it yourself." ⁵Throwing down the pieces of silver in the temple, he departed; and he went and hanged himself. ⁶But the chief priests, taking the pieces of silver, said, "It is not lawful to put them into the treasury, since they are blood money." ⁷After conferring together, they used them to buy the potter's field as a place to bury foreigners. ⁸For this reason that field has been called the Field of Blood to this day. ⁹Then was fulfilled what had been spoken through the prophet Jeremiah, "And they took the thirty pieces of silver, the price of the one on whom a price had been set, on whom some of the people of Israel had set a price, ¹⁰and they gave them for the potter's field, as the Lord commanded me."

¹¹Now Jesus stood before the governor; and the governor asked him, "Are you the King of the Jews?" Jesus said, "You say so." ¹²But when he was accused by the chief priests and elders, he did not answer. ¹³Then Pilate said to him, "Do you not hear how many accusations they make against you?" ¹⁴But he gave him no answer, not even to a single charge, so that the

governor was greatly amazed. ¹⁵Now at the festival the governor was accustomed to release a prisoner for the crowd, anyone whom they wanted. ¹⁶At that time they had a notorious prisoner, called Jesus Barabbas. ¹⁷So after they had gathered, Pilate said to them, "Whom do you want me to release for you, Jesus Barabbas or Jesus who is called the Messiah?" ¹⁸For he realized that it was out of jealousy that they had handed him over. ¹⁹While he was sitting on the judgment seat, his wife sent word to him, "Have nothing to do with that innocent man, for today I have suffered a great deal because of a dream about him." ²⁰Now the chief priests and the elders persuaded the crowds to ask for Barabbas and to have Jesus killed. ²¹The governor again said to them, "Which of the two do you want me to release for you?" And they said, "Barabbas." ²²Pilate said to them, "Then what should I do with Jesus who is called the Messiah?" All of them said, "Let him be crucified!" ²³Then he asked, "Why, what evil has he done?" But they shouted all the more, "Let him be crucified!"

Reflection

"Ah, holy Jesus, how has thou offended?"

This phrase in a treasured hymn asks the question we all wonder: Why is this evidently guiltless teacher, healer, and proclaimer of the kingdom of heaven condemned to death? Readers and hearers of Matthew's Gospel know that Jesus' disciples come to believe that he is the promised Messiah, the Christ, and Son of God. But now he is found deserving of death by the supreme Jewish council and handed over to the Roman governor to carry out the execution. Evidently only this occupying foreign power has the authority to enforce capital punishment. In one of the most dramatic scenes in all of human history, this bound, mocked, and seemingly powerless individual is brought before the judgment seat of the representative of the world's most powerful government.

Before the trial, however, another thread is drawn to its endpoint in the story, as we hear of the death of Jesus' betrayer. Only in Matthew's Gospel do we learn of Judas' remorse and suicide.

All four of our gospels present their versions of the trial before Pilate. Matthew emphasizes Pilate's reluctance to take responsibility for Jesus' death by offering (as in the other gospels) to release Jesus in exchange for the "notorious prisoner" Barabbas, asking with regard to Jesus, "Why, what evil has he done?" Matthew is the only gospel to tell of Pilate's wife's dream and her plea that Pilate "have nothing to do with that innocent man." But, stirred up by Jewish officials, the crowds call out for Jesus' crucifixion.

The Rt. Rev. Frederick Borsch
Chair of Anglican Studies,
Lutheran Theological Seminary at Philadelphia
Philadelphia, Pennsylvania

Question

"Ah, holy Jesus, how has thou offended?" Can you imagine being in Pilate's shoes?

Prayer

Holy Jesus, we want to be innocent of suffering, but we are not. Be with us as we share in love's compassion. Amen.

Matthew 27:24-44

²⁴So when Pilate saw that he could do nothing, but rather that a riot was beginning, he took some water and washed his hands before the crowd, saying, "I am innocent of this man's blood; see to it yourselves." ²⁵Then the people as a whole answered, "His blood be on us and on our children!"

²⁶So he released Barabbas for them; and after flogging Jesus, he handed him over to be crucified. ²⁷Then the soldiers of the governor took Jesus into the governor's headquarters, and they gathered the whole cohort around him. ²⁸They stripped him and put a scarlet robe on him, ²⁹and after twisting some thorns into a crown, they put it on his head. They put a reed in his right hand and knelt before him and mocked him, saying, "Hail, King of the Jews!" ³⁰They spat on him, and took the reed and struck him on the head. ³¹After mocking him, they stripped him of the robe and put his own clothes on him. Then they led him away to crucify him. ³²As they went out, they came upon a man from Cyrene named Simon; they compelled this man to carry his cross.

³³And when they came to a place called Golgotha (which means Place of a Skull), ³⁴they offered him wine to drink, mixed with gall; but when he tasted it, he would not drink it. ³⁵And when they had crucified him, they divided his clothes among themselves by casting lots; ³⁶then they sat down there and kept watch over him. ³⁷Over his head they put the charge against him, which read, "This is Jesus, the King of the Jews." ³⁸Then two bandits were crucified with

him, one on his right and one on his left. [39]Those who passed by derided him, shaking their heads [40]and saying, "You who would destroy the temple and build it in three days, save yourself! If you are the Son of God, come down from the cross." [41]In the same way the chief priests also, along with the scribes and elders, were mocking him, saying, [42]"He saved others; he cannot save himself. He is the King of Israel; let him come down from the cross now, and we will believe in him. [43]He trusts in God; let God deliver him now, if he wants to; for he said, 'I am God's Son.'" [44]The bandits who were crucified with him also taunted him in the same way.

Reflection

Matthew's Gospel continues to emphasize Pilate's reluctance to be responsible for Jesus' crucifixion as he washes his hands before the crowd, saying, "I am innocent of this man's blood." To this the people respond, "His blood be on us and on our children."

Who then is truly innocent? Who then is guilty? In versions of Luke's Gospel (23:34), we hear Jesus' words, "Father, forgive them, for they know not what they are doing." In any event, it is a tragic misunderstanding to hear the people's cry "his blood be on us and on our children" as some lasting and unforgiven responsibility for the one whose blood was shed "for the forgiveness of sins." A far better Christian understanding pictures the forgiven Christian at the foot of the cross, crying (in the words of a hymn) "who brought this upon you?/I crucified you."

Crucifixion was designed to be a form of torture as well as death. The dying man, in effect finally suffocating from his own sagging weight, could be mocked and derided. In the words of another hymn, "Sometimes it makes me tremble, tremble, tremble" to look upon this tortured death as an incarnation of all the world's savagery and suffering. In this story, the irony is made graphic: Jesus is, indeed, king—if a different kind of king. He, whom God does not deliver, is, indeed, God's Son, to whom one prays "to mourn thee well-beloved/yet thank thee for thy death."

The Rt. Rev. Frederick Borsch
Chair of Anglican Studies,
Lutheran Theological Seminary at Philadelphia
Philadelphia, Pennsylvania

A Journey with Matthew

Questions

Who is responsible for Jesus' crucifixion? Who is innocent?

Does the story of the crucifixion (in the words of the hymn) cause you to "tremble" and "yet thank thee for thy death?" How?

Prayer

Blessed Jesus, look on your trembling and grateful people. Help us to share in faith that suffering may lead to love. Amen.

Matthew 27:45-66

⁴⁵From noon on, darkness came over the whole land until three in the afternoon. ⁴⁶And about three o'clock Jesus cried with a loud voice, "Eli, Eli, lema sabachthani?" that is, "My God, my God, why have you forsaken me?" ⁴⁷When some of the bystanders heard it, they said, "This man is calling for Elijah." ⁴⁸At once one of them ran and got a sponge, filled it with sour wine, put it on a stick, and gave it to him to drink. ⁴⁹But the others said, "Wait, let us see whether Elijah will come to save him."

⁵⁰Then Jesus cried again with a loud voice and breathed his last. ⁵¹At that moment the curtain of the temple was torn in two, from top to bottom. The earth shook, and the rocks were split. ⁵²The tombs also were opened, and many bodies of the saints who had fallen asleep were raised. ⁵³After his resurrection they came out of the tombs and entered the holy city and appeared to many. ⁵⁴Now when the centurion and those with him, who were keeping watch over Jesus, saw the earthquake and what took place, they were terrified and said, "Truly this man was God's Son!" ⁵⁵Many women were also there, looking on from a distance; they had followed Jesus from Galilee and had provided for him. ⁵⁶Among them were Mary Magdalene, and Mary the mother of James and Joseph, and the mother of the sons of Zebedee.

⁵⁷When it was evening, there came a rich man from Arimathea, named Joseph, who was also a disciple of Jesus. ⁵⁸He

went to Pilate and asked for the body of Jesus; then Pilate ordered it to be given to him. [59]So Joseph took the body and wrapped it in a clean linen cloth [60]and laid it in his own new tomb, which he had hewn in the rock. He then rolled a great stone to the door of the tomb and went away. [61]Mary Magdalene and the other Mary were there, sitting opposite the tomb. [62]The next day, that is, after the day of Preparation, the chief priests and the Pharisees gathered before Pilate [63]and said, "Sir, we remember what that impostor said while he was still alive, 'After three days I will rise again.' [64]Therefore command the tomb to be made secure until the third day; otherwise his disciples may go and steal him away, and tell the people, 'He has been raised from the dead,' and the last deception would be worse than the first." [65]Pilate said to them, "You have a guard of soldiers; go, make it as secure as you can." [66]So they went with the guard and made the tomb secure by sealing the stone.

Reflection

In the crucifixion and death of Jesus, God chooses to reconcile the world to God's own self. "Lord Jesus Christ," we pray, "you stretched out your arms of love on the hard wood of the cross that everyone might come within the reach of your saving embrace" (*The Book of Common Prayer*, p. 101). This is the gospel—the epic Good News—that every person, and indeed the whole creation, has been reconciled to God.

Gratitude and compassion compel us to take this news out beyond the beautiful liturgies of the church, into a world riven by violence in God's name, terror, deprivation in the shadow of affluence, pandemic anxiety and depression. The world needs to hear this news. Badly.

George MacLeod, founder of the Iona Community in Scotland, is well-known for his proclamation that the cross be raised not only on the steeple of the church but also at the center of the market place. MacLeod wrote, "Jesus was not crucified in a cathedral between two candles, but on a cross between two thieves; on the town garbage heap; at a crossroad of politics so cosmopolitan that they had to write his title in Hebrew and in Latin and in Greek;…at the kind of place where cynics talk smut, and thieves curse, and soldiers gamble. Because that is where he died, and that is what he died about."

And that is where Christ's people ought to be, and what Christ's people ought to be about.

The Rev. David R. Anderson
Writer and Rector of St. Luke's Parish
Darien, Connecticut

A Journey with Matthew

Question

God entrusts to us the ministry of reconciliation. Where can you—and only you—take this Good News?

Prayer

Send us, Lord, into an aching world with the Good News that heals and reconciles, in the merciful name of Christ. Amen.

Matthew 28:1-20

28 After the sabbath, as the first day of the week was dawning, Mary Magdalene and the other Mary went to see the tomb. ²And suddenly there was a great earthquake; for an angel of the Lord, descending from heaven, came and rolled back the stone and sat on it. ³His appearance was like lightning, and his clothing white as snow. ⁴For fear of him the guards shook and became like dead men. ⁵But the angel said to the women, "Do not be afraid; I know that you are looking for Jesus who was crucified. ⁶He is not here; for he has been raised, as he said. Come, see the place where he lay. ⁷Then go quickly and tell his disciples, 'He has been raised from the dead, and indeed he is going ahead of you to Galilee; there you will see him.' This is my message for you." ⁸So they left the tomb quickly with fear and great joy, and ran to tell his disciples. ⁹Suddenly Jesus met them and said, "Greetings!" And they came to him, took hold of his feet, and worshiped him. ¹⁰Then Jesus said to them, "Do not be afraid; go and tell my brothers to go to Galilee; there they will see me."

¹¹While they were going, some of the guard went into the city and told the chief priests everything that had happened. ¹²After the priests had assembled with the elders, they devised a plan to give a large sum of money to the soldiers, ¹³telling them, "You must say, 'His disciples came by night and stole him away while we were asleep.' ¹⁴If this comes to the governor's ears, we will satisfy him and keep you out of trouble." ¹⁵So they took the

money and did as they were directed. And this story is still told among the Jews to this day.

[16]Now the eleven disciples went to Galilee, to the mountain to which Jesus had directed them. [17]When they saw him, they worshiped him; but some doubted. [18]And Jesus came and said to them, "All authority in heaven and on earth has been given to me. [19]Go therefore and make disciples of all nations, baptizing them in the name of the Father and of the Son and of the Holy Spirit, [20]and teaching them to obey everything that I have commanded you. And remember, I am with you always, to the end of the age."

Reflection

Easter is God's answer to the tyrants who presume to rule this world, and no evangelist makes this clearer than Matthew.

In the final line of yesterday's reading, the powers that be have set a guard to prevent Jesus' disciples from stealing the body and trumpeting a "resurrection." For insurance, they made the tomb secure by sealing the stone.

You have to laugh a little, seeing these small, fearful people, coming with their mortar mixers and trowels, slapping concrete in the cracks around the stone and laying it on thick. No army could roll away this stone. They check their weapons and have a leisurely smoke.

They were ready for petty grave robbers. They weren't prepared for an earthquake. The ground shook, and the angel descended, rolled back the stone, and the wisecracking guards "shook and became like dead men."

The earthquake is God's sign that the Resurrection is not something private and personal. It's a cosmic event; it's a shake-up of the old world order. Jesus' Resurrection means that the forces of death and oppression are no longer in charge. The forces of hate and cruelty have been put on notice.

"The resurrection stories," says Bishop N. T. Wright in the book, *The Resurrection*, "do not say Jesus is raised, therefore we're going to heaven, or therefore we're going to be raised. They say Jesus is raised, therefore God's new creation has begun and we've got a job to do."

That Easter job takes us wherever the powers of death pretend to rule.

The Rev. David R. Anderson
Writer and Rector of St. Luke's Parish
Darien, Connecticut

Question _____

How can you equip yourself in prayer and find supportive friends who can help you to confront the powers of death?

Prayer _____

The powers of death have done their worst, but Christ their legions hath dispersed. Alleluia. Amen.

About the Authors

The Rev. David R. Anderson is a writer and priest, serving as rector of St. Luke's Parish in Darien, Connecticut. He is the author of *Breakfast Epiphanies* (Beacon Press, 2002) and *Losing Your Faith, Finding Your Soul: The Passage to New Life When Old Beliefs Die* (Convergent Books, 2013). He blogs at www.findingyoursoul.com. *Days 49-50.*

The Rt. Rev. Frederick Borsch has served as professor of New Testament literature, Dean and President of the Church Divinity School of the Pacific, Dean of the Chapel with the rank of professor of religion at Princeton University, and as the Bishop of Los Angeles. He has taught New Testament studies at several other universities and divinity schools, most recently at the Lutheran Theological Seminary at Philadelphia. *Days 47-48.*

The Rt. Rev. Paul Butler is Bishop of Durham, having served previously as Bishop of Southwell & Nottingham and Southampton. His key interests are his family, ministry alongside children, East Africa, and in all things, making Jesus Christ known. *Days 29-30.*

Bo Cox has written inspirational and down-to-earth meditations for Forward Movement for nearly twenty years. His first set of reflections were published in *Forward Day by Day* in 1995, when he was still serving a life sentence for first-degree murder. He has written for nine months of *Forward Day by Day*, meditations for Lent, and a collection of essays for *God is Not In the Thesaurus: Stories from an Oklahoma Prison*. His newest book is *I Will, With God's Help* (Forward Movement, 2014). Released from prison in 2003, Bo leads therapeutic activities at a psychiatric hospital. He also serves as a consultant to St. Albans School in Washington, D.C. *Days 13-14.*

The Rev. Barbara Cawthorne Crafton is an Episcopal priest and writer. She is best known for The Almost-Daily eMo, a devotional essay read by thousands worldwide. Her next book, *The Courage To Grow Old*, will be published in 2014. *Days 45-46.*

The Rt. Rev. Michael Curry is Bishop of the Diocese of North Carolina. Throughout his ministry, he has been a passionate advocate for the poor and for children. A well-regarded preacher, he is the author of *Crazy Christians*, a book of his sermons. *Days 27-28.*

The Rt. Rev. Clifton Daniel served as Bishop of the Diocese of East Carolina from 1996-2013 and now serves as Bishop of the Diocese of Pennsylvania. A native of North Carolina, he is a graduate of the University of North Carolina at Chapel Hill and Virginia Theological Seminary. He and his wife have three grown daughters. *Days 3-4.*

The Rt. Rev. Mary Gray-Reeves is Bishop of the Diocese of El Camino Real in California. She is author of *Unearthing My Religion*, and coauthor of *The Hospitality of God*. She is engaged in the twenty-first-century work of the Church to share Jesus and his way of grace in the world. *Days 25-26.*

The Rev. Scott Gunn is Executive Director of Forward Movement, an organization promoting discipleship in The Episcopal Church, based in Cincinnati, Ohio. He travels widely as a preacher and speaker, and he blogs at www.sevenwholedays.org. *Days 5-6.*

The Rev. Daniel R. Heischman is Executive Director of the National Association of Episcopal Schools. Formerly college chaplain at Trinity College in Hartford, Connecticut, and Upper School Head at St. Albans School in Washington, D.C., he began his ministry at St. Paul's Episcopal Church in Englewood, New Jersey, and continued as chaplain and head of the religion department at Trinity School in New York City. *Days 31-32.*

The Rt. Rev. Graham James is Bishop of Norwich. He began his ministry serving new housing areas in Peterborough, England and then Welwyn Garden City, north of London. He became chaplain to the Archbishop of Canterbury in 1987 and became a bishop in his native county of Cornwall in 1993. In his ministry, he has had particular responsibility for ministerial selection and training in the Church of England, relationships with the media, and the role of the Church in rural life. *Days 33-34.*

The Very Rev. Cynthia Briggs Kittredge, Dean and President of Seminary of the Southwest since June 2013, served as academic dean of the seminary since 2010 and professor of New Testament since she joined the faculty in 1999. She holds degrees from Williams College and Harvard Divinity School, where she earned a Th.D. in 1996. She was ordained priest in 1985 and is canonically resident in the Diocese of Texas. She has served as assisting clergy at Episcopal Church of the Good Shepherd since 1999. *Days 39-40.*

The Most Rev. Bolly anak Lapok is the fourth Metropolitan Archbishop and Primate of the Anglican Church of the Province of South East Asia as well as the Bishop of Kuching. An ethnic

Iban, he is the first primate of the province from Sarawak. He has served as the Chairman of the Association of Churches in Sarawak since 2009. *Days 23-24.*

The Very Rev. Tracey Lind is Dean of Trinity Cathedral in Cleveland, Ohio. As an urban priest and city planner, her ministry includes work for environmental and social justice, interfaith relations, sustainable urban planning, and diversity in The Episcopal Church. A trustee of the Church Pension Fund, she is also an exhibiting photographer and author of *Interrupted by God: Glimpses from the Edge* (The Pilgrim Press, 2004). *Days 37-38.*

Stephen Lyon has been involved in different ministries in the Anglican Church for over thirty-five years. In 2009 he was asked to coordinate a project for the worldwide Anglican Communion. This project, *The Bible in the Life of the Church*, seeks to encourage a deeper engagement with scripture and to offer resources to help people achieve that. He lives in London with his wife. *Days 17-18.*

The Very Rev. Ian S. Markham, PhD is the Dean and President of Virginia Theological Seminary and associate priest at St. Paul's Episcopal Church, Alexandria, Virginia. He has degrees from the King's College London, the University of Cambridge, and the University of Exeter. He is the author and editor of twenty-four books, including *Against Atheism* (Wiley Blackwell, 2010) and *Liturgical Life Principles* (Church Publishing, 2009). *Days 1-2.*

The Very Rev. Kate Moorehead is Dean of St. John's Cathedral in Jacksonville, Florida, and the author of four books: *Between Two Worlds, Organic God, Get Over Yourself,* and *Resurrecting Easter.* She and her husband have three boys. Her writings also can be found at motherkate.blogspot.com. *Days 11-12.*

The Most Rev. Barry Morgan has been the Archbishop of Wales since 2003. In 1993 he became the Bishop of Bangor and then, in 1999, the Bishop of Llandaff. He has served on the central committee of the World Council of Churches and on the Primates Standing Committee of the Anglican Communion. He was a member of the Lambeth Commission, which produced the Windsor Report 2004. He has written books on various subjects, including the poetry of R. S. Thomas. He is currently pro-chancellor of the University of Wales. *Days 7-8.*

The Rev. Riaz Mubarak has served as a priest for fourteen years in the Diocese of Peshawar in the Church of Pakistan. He provides pastoral care, conducts interfaith dialogues, and manages free medical camps. *Days 35-36.*

The Rev. Sam Portaro is Episcopal Chaplain Emeritus to The University of Chicago. He serves on the faculty of CREDO and is the author of several books, most recently *Transforming Vocation* (Church Publishing, 2008). *Days 9-10.*

Jeremiah Sierra is a writer and editor. He is the Managing Editor for Trinity Wall Street and writes occasionally for Forward Movement and the Episcopal Church Foundation's Vital Practices. *Days 21-22.*

The Rev. Becca Stevens is an Episcopal priest and founder of Magdalene House, residential communities of women who have survived prostitution, trafficking, and addiction. She founded Thistle Farms in 2001, which currently employs nearly fifty residents and graduates, and houses a natural body care line, a paper and sewing studio, and the Thistle Stop Café. A prolific writer, she has authored ten books. Her latest, *The Way of Tea & Justice: Rescuing the World's Favorite Beverage from its Violent History*, releases in 2014. *Days 19-20.*

Ray Suarez is the host of the daily news program *Inside Story* on Al Jazeera America TV. A lifelong Episcopalian, he is most recently the author of *Latino Americans: The 500 Year Legacy That Shaped a Nation* (Penguin/Celebra, 2013). He works and worships in Washington, D.C. *Days 43-44.*

The Rev. Hillary T. West serves at Epiphany Episcopal Church in Herndon, Virginia. She is serving faithfully with a remnant flock called to use their gifts to rebuild and grow a caring community in a vibrant suburb of Washington, D.C. *Days 15-16.*

The Rev. Marek P. Zabriskie is the Rector of St. Thomas Episcopal Church in Fort Washington, Pennsylvania, and founder and director of the Center for Biblical Studies, which promotes The Bible Challenge globally. He previously served at St. James's Episcopal Church in Richmond, Virginia, and at St. George's Episcopal Church in Nashville, Tennessee. He edited *The Bible Challenge* published by Forward Movement and will have a book coming out in 2014 called *Doing the Bible Better: Unleashing the Bible for Transformation in the Episcopal Church. Days 41-42.*

Acknowledgements

There are so many people to thank for helping launch The Bible Challenge and who have encouraged its rapid growth across the United States and around the world. It would take a small book to cite all of them. Let me mention a few.

I will be always grateful to the Rev. Frank Allen, who inspired me to return to the scriptures in a deeper way and to read the entire Bible in the course of a year. It was just the medicine that I needed for my own soul.

I am extremely grateful to Rowan Williams, 104th Archbishop of Canterbury, who has been a friend and a supporter and eagerly agreed to serve on the international Advisory Board of the Center for Biblical Studies, which helps to share and promote The Bible Challenge globally.

Professors Walter Brueggemann, perhaps the greatest Old Testament scholar alive, and Harry Attridge, former Dean of the Yale Divinity School, jumped aboard early and helped The Bible Challenge succeed and make an impact. They continue to serve on our national Advisory Board.

The Rev. Scott Gunn, Executive Director of Forward Movement, is an incredibly innovative thinker and an enormous gift to the Church. He has offered inspirational insights for our ministry. His support—and that of Forward Movement and Richelle Thompson, Managing Editor—has been invaluable. It is a joy to work with Scott and Richelle.

I wish to thank our contributors who have taken time from their busy schedules to write insightful meditations and thoughtful questions and prayers for each day of *A Journey with Matthew*. Each of them is a gift to the Church. We are honored to include their wisdom.

Finally, I wish to thank my wife, Mims, and our daughters, Emily, Marguerite, and Isabelle, who have allowed me to devote an enormous amount of time to The Bible Challenge in my free hours, and to our church, St. Thomas Episcopal Church, a special spiritual home with a faithful congregation that is walking side by side on a journey of faith, with Christ leading the way.

With blessings and prayers,

The Rev. Marek P. Zabriskie